Here's what others are saying about

The Day after Graduation

"Your book has been a fascinating read.
I think it will be a fabulous gift."

—*Jodie Raddatz, Librarian*

"I wish I'd had this book when I graduated from school
in the sixties. The information would have been priceless."

—*Dr. Chris Wolf*

"This is a "how to" book a dean or graduate will learn from!"

—*Mary Brabeck, Dean of the Steinhardt School of Education, NYU*

"Excellent. I would like to refer to your book as a good buy—one every parent should
purchase for their children."

—*Micheal Kalscheur, Home Schooler*

"I found its message to be both practical and inspiring and thus very useful for graduates at all levels. With so many of our teenagers and young adults confused by the mixed messages society and the media send them, this is precisely the type of idea we need to spread: that we are in control of our life outcomes and that our actions have consequences for ourselves and those around us."

—*Joel L. Klein, Chancellor*
New York City Department of Education

The Day after Graduation

What Your Parents and Teachers Did Not Teach You in School

REVISED EDITION

Francis Brazeau

Circle of Life Books

Bonita Springs, Florida • South Bend, Indiana

Illustrations by Gary Houser

First printing 2009

ISBN 978-0-9787536-1-0

LCCN 2009924235

ATTENTION CORPORATIONS, UNIVERSITIES, COLLEGES, AND PROFESSIONAL ORGANIZATIONS: Quantity discounts are available on bulk purchases of this book for educational, gift purposes, or as premiums for increasing magazine subscriptions or renewals. Special books or book excerpts can also be created to fit specific needs. For information, please contact Circle of Life Books, 5223 Monticello Court, South Bend, IN 46614; 574-291-0088.

I dedicate this to my wife Eleanor,

who has made my life such a pleasure.

We Don't Owe
Our People
a Brighter Future—

But We Do Owe
Our Future
a Brighter People

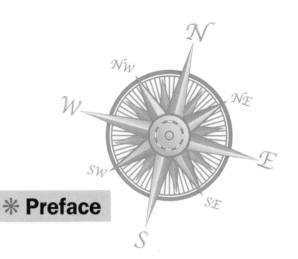

✳ Preface

THE YEAR WAS 1951, and my wife, daughter, and I had moved to South Bend, Indiana, to open a franchise under the auspices of the Accounting Corp of America. We were one of the first to sell this type of service to corporations and individuals, using IBM equipment to assist them in their accounting needs.

Shortly thereafter, I joined the Elmer Wheeler Sales Group and took a two-hour, fourteen-week class in salesmanship to learn the nuances of selling. Elmer always said, "Don't sell the steak; sell the sizzle," and we learned to say, "Boy, am I enthusiastic!" Today, in my eighty-seventh year, I repeat the latter ten times a day and thus have never lost my lust for life, nor my enthusiasm. I have been there and done that.

My wife Eleanor and I were spending a quiet evening at home discussing a myriad of subjects—history, politics, and current events, to name a few—and then ended the evening talking about the direction our education system was going, and she said, "Why don't you write a book?" Nothing more was said, but a few days later I picked up a legal pad and started jotting down notes from our conversation, which became the precursor to this book.

After a year of research, hours of interviews with high school and college students, academics, and businessmen, deleting and rewriting, and changing thoughts many times along the way, the book came together. Decision making was a constant part of the process. Unfortunately, I could not verify some items, especially in chapter 9, as they were written many years ago.

It is my sincere hope that you, the reader, will find this book educational, interesting, a fun read, and a companion for the rest of your life.

—*Francis Brazeau*

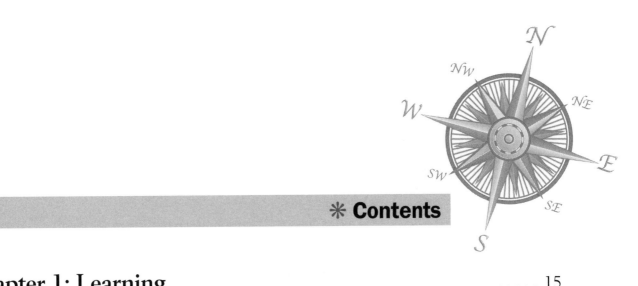

✳ Contents

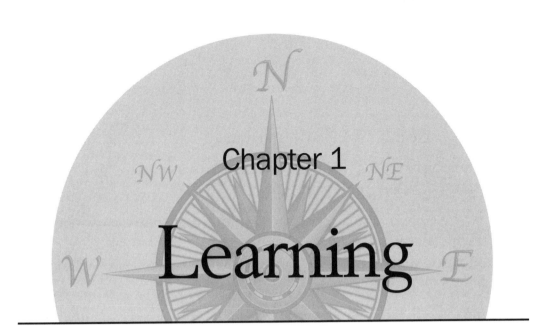

Chapter 1

Learning

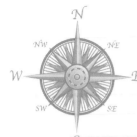

KNOWLEDGE IS ENERGY for the mind.

From birth throughout life, one is constantly learning. You learn something every day, whether you realize it or not.

There are numerous opportunities to enhance one's knowledge, by attending lectures, taking classes, traveling, reading books and newspapers, participating in discussion groups, listening to the radio, and watching TV. The list is endless.

How much you learn by any of the above means is up to you. If you really set your mind to learning something, by eliminating as many distractions as possible, you are much more likely to retain it.

You must also have a goal in life, a plan for what you would like to do and be in the future. Circumstances may change these plans and change your goals—but don't give up, as nobody ever promised you the good life from birth to death. It is definitely up to you, because you and you alone are responsible for your actions throughout your life.

Why Should Anyone Read This Book?

1. Three little words, "in the beginning," so simple yet so powerful: From this day forward, everything you do will be "in the beginning." An old Chinese proverb states that "A thousand mile journey begins with a single step."

2. By learning about the subjects in this book and putting them into practice in your daily life, you can save money.

3. If you are already familiar with these subjects, you may wish to teach a friend.

4. From the time you awaken until you climb into bed, you start "in the beginning" of the day. You can work with diligence or just sneak by in whatever endeavor you have undertaken.

5. So why not get up with a smile, greet your cohorts graciously, help whoever needs help, and go home to your family, knowing you have done your job well? Everyone you come into contact with will say, "There goes a good person."

6. In the following pages, you are given a bird's-eye view of things you will face on your journey through life. Read and reread this book until you fully understand all the chapters and keep them firmly imprinted in your mind.

7. By doing so, you will not only save money from the knowledge you have acquired but also earn the respect of your peers in future business dealings. Recommendation: Develop good reading habits; read at least one book a month for the rest of your life, not just love stories or "whodunits" but autobiographies, biographies, histories of our world, especially of the US. Once you start, it will be hard to quit reading.

What I Didn't Learn from My Teachers or My Parents

The year is 2008, and on August 28th I turned eighty-seven. So what's the big deal? No big deal, as I have been blessed with good health, had a wonderful mother (my father died when I was four months short of my sixth birthday), and grew up with three sisters and a brother, all younger than I. Now, as a father of six daughters and with a multitude of friends across the country, my cup is full and running over.

Watching my children grow up, along with my children's friends, I became aware that business subjects weren't included in their school curricula. Students were sent out into the real world without learning much about budgeting, insurance, saving, investing, and so on. Some schools are exceptions, but overall we are doing our children a great disservice by not adding a general business class to the curriculum. This course should be required for all high school students to complete before they are given a diploma.

I am writing this book for the young people of America, whom I feel have been short-changed on matters they should have learned long before their high school graduation.

We are all given X minutes of life. No one knows what his or her X is. Some have very few. How we use these precious moments, which turn into hours, days, months, and years, is somewhat up to each person, but why do some have to wait years to learn what they could have learned while still young and go out into the real world without more business savvy? The answer is quite simple.

The following is a recap of one person's learning experience, *mine*.

How many times have I said to myself, why didn't someone warn me? Why didn't I study harder in high school and college? Why do some students find learning so easy whereas others must work much harder to acquire the same knowledge? Vince Lombardi, former football coach of the world champion Green Bay Packers, said, "We are not born equal, but, in fact, very much unequal." Some of us are born with an abundance of native intelligence, which develops as the years go by; others have a gift for athletics, while others still have mathematical or scientific minds. Why is Mother Nature so unfair?

Here is another observation worth recalling. American author and humorist Mark Twain said, "When I was sixteen years old, I thought my old man was the dumbest man in the world; when I became twenty-one, I wondered how he got so smart in five years."

When I was in the eighth grade, my mother was my teacher. The school enrollment was about thirty-six students in each grade, half from the village of Coleman, Wisconsin, and the other half from the country surrounding our town. The high school consisted of a large home room, containing about one hundred students, and six other rooms for English, math, geography, history, chemistry, and typing. Yup, that was it.

No one in the 1930s and early 1940s could dream of coming events, atom bombs, air flights faster than the speed of sound, the Internet, TV, satellite radio, fast and beautiful autos, air conditioning, or trans-Atlantic air travel. Looking at our achievements, especially in science and medicine, we wondered, when we exploded an atom bomb and when men landed on the moon, "How far can we advance?"

As time goes by, you will appreciate more and more the knowledge you have acquired. Your financial rewards will increase accordingly, and the harder you work, the more successful you will become.

Why Don't We Learn a Little about You?

The following pages are for your self-analysis.

Complete the questionnaire as directed and, when you finish, check your score and set goals for improving your weak points.

From time to time, check and review how much you have improved. You may be pleasantly surprised at your progress.

Give the test to your friends, and get their reaction. Ask them whether they agree with your self-analysis.

Learning more about yourself will help you learn more about your friends and business associates.

Self-Analysis

What self-help can do:

This self-analysis chart gives you an opportunity to check yourself on personal and business characteristics that can help you achieve greater success.

You cannot think long and seriously about yourself, your personal characteristics, your successes and failures, your strong points and your weak ones, your personal assets and liabilities, your real earning capacity, and your future possibilities without discovering some things you can do to improve yourself immediately and finding some new ways of "cashing in" to better advantage on your experience, training, and everything you are or possess.

If you will read and reread the questions slowly and methodically, you may suddenly realize their importance and start to improve your image in the eyes of others and in your own eyes. About thirty days from now, answer the questions again and note your improvement.

Today in the US there is a terrible abuse of the English language. The words "you know" are used as filler by tired brains that cannot seem to articulate a coherent thought and instead rely on these two monotonous words that do not tell the audience anything and are, I might add, a very poor use of our beautiful language.

Another aggravating expression is "ah…ah…ah," etc., which in essence says, "I am confused and don't know what to say."

If you are guilty of these abuses and would like to stop using them, here is a simple but 99 percent successful way of stopping these habits. Try this great antidote.

Take a small container and place it on your kitchen table and every time you catch yourself saying, "You know" or "ah…ah," place a quarter in the container. Before the container is full, you probably will have stopped these two nasty habits and should have enough money to take a friend out to dinner. Your author would be pleased to hear of your results.

How to Grade

Grade yourself in response to each question on a scale from 0 to 10. If you believe you are where you should be, give yourself 10 points; if you're only so-so, give yourself 5 points; and if you're not at all where you should be, give yourself a 0.

Just be objective and apply ordinary common sense. Consider what a discriminating person in full possession of the facts would give you.

When you have graded yourself on each of the one hundred questions, add the grades and place the sum in the proper place at the end of the column. Divide the sum total by 10 for your percentage of efficiency.

I. Appearance

1. Is your expression pleasant? _____

2. Clothes spotless and pressed, shoes shined? _____

3. Are your clothes selected with taste/style, fit, color, harmony? _____

4. Do you look like the master of yourself? _____

5. Are your manners pleasant and friendly? _____

6. Do you correct all appearance deficiencies? _____

II. Health

7. Is your health a business asset? _____

8. Is your health as important as money? _____

9. Do you observe the simple health rules for eating, drinking, breathing, and exercising? _____

10. Is your power of endurance above average? _____

11. Have you lost any school days or work days this year due to illness? _____

III. Fearlessness

12. Are you at ease before strangers or superiors? _____

13. Are you conscious of the new courage that results from acquired power? _____

14. Do you follow your own convictions? _____

15. Have you eliminated all fear of the future? _____

16. Do you meet problems squarely, without evasion? _____

17. Do you use knowledge to banish fear? _____

IV. Self-Confidence

18. Are you sure of yourself at all times? _____

19. Do you use and apply your knowledge? _____

20. Do you start things with confidence rather than with doubt and cold feet? _____

21. Are you confident about your own judgment? _____

22. Are your actions the result of your self-confidence? _____

23. Are you able to inspire confidence in others? _____

V. Ambition

24. Is your life's aim big enough for your ability? _____

25. Do you back your ambition with decisive action? _____

26. Do you plan each day to advance another step? _____

27. Do you study the best ways for personal advancement? _____

28. Do you take full advantage of opportunities? _____

29. Are you eager to do well in life? _____

30. Would fulfillment of your ambitions make this world a better place? _____

VI. Will Power

31. Is your will power trained for decisive action? _____

32. Can you shoulder responsibility without worry? _____

33. Do you control your temper and words? _____

34. Can you shed nonessential details? _____

35. Do you make enough time for self-development? _____

36. Is your will like "high-tempered steel"? _____

37. Is daily practice of your will power a habit? _____

VII. Concentration

38. Do you train yourself to concentrate at will? _____

39. Are surroundings picked to favor concentration? _____

40. Does business study get undivided attention? _____

41. Can you concentrate for a long period? _____

42. Are you developing a clear, accurate, hard-thinking business mind? _____

43. Do you really "think" rather than kid yourself to believe you think? _____

VIII. Suggestion

44. Do you seek the value of positive ideas? _____

45. Do you avoid negative suggestions? _____

46. Is indifference allowed to hinder progress? _____

47. Do your manners show positive suggestions? _____

48. Do you use the power of self-suggestion? _____

IX. Tact

49. Do you get along well with most people? _____

50. Do you try to "lead" rather than "boss"? _____

51. Do you avoid loss of temper and sarcasm? _____

52. Do you avoid hasty remarks that hurt others? _____

53. Do you always practice the highest courtesy? _____

54. Do you always express appreciation when due? _____

X. Interest

55. Are you deeply interested in your own work? _____

56. Do you make careful daily observation of your work to improve it? _____

57. Are you interested in the human problems of business management? _____

58. Do you observe people's features and study their characteristics? _____

59. Do you endeavor to read people's thoughts to anticipate their needs? _____

60. Have you an interest in problems of modern business? _____

61. Are you yourself your greatest object of constructive study? _____

XI. Sincerity

62. Is your word as good as a bond? _____

63. Do you have high ideals of life and service? _____

64. Is your work interesting rather than routine? _____

65. Do you stand loyally by your deserving friends? _____

66. Are you sincere even though it sometimes results in apparent disadvantages? _____

67. Are you honest for reasons other than because "it pays"? _____

68. Do you practice what you demand from others? _____

XII. Alertness

69. Can you understand the viewpoints of others? _____

70. Are you quick to understand instructions? _____

71. Are you known as a wide-awake person? _____

XIII. Memory

72. Is your memory excellent? _____

73. Do you train your memory for improvement? _____

74. Do you remember names as easily as faces? _____

75. Can you forget non-essential facts? _____

76. Do you depend on trained memory power rather than short-cut-methods? _____

77. Do you consciously combat every tendency to absentmindedness? _____

XIV. Effective Speech

78. Do you speak without hesitation? _____

79. Are your ideas clearly and logically organized? _____

80. Are you master of yourself when talking to a group of people? _____

81. While eating with superiors, are you at ease? _____

82. Do you convince people? _____

83. Do you secure the desired action from people? _____

XV. Initiative

84. Do you seek opportunities to better yourself? _____

85. Do you make plans to realize your goal? _____

86. Do you have to be directed less than the average person?   _____

87. Do you make constructive suggestions freely?   _____

88. Are you systematically developing your power of constructive imagination?   _____

89. Are you right now thinking of how to profit by use of this chart?   _____

90. Are you able to meet new situations with dispatch and confidence?   _____

91. Does experience prove your ideas practical?   _____

XVI. Reliability

92. Are you known as a person who "gets things done"?   _____

93. Are you trustworthy in little things?   _____

94. Is your credit good at all times?   _____

95. Do you keep your promises and appointments?   _____

96. Are you reliable in all of your work?   _____

97. Is your judgment so sound and reliable that it is sought by others?   _____

98. Do you establish your "reliability" as thoroughly as your "ability"?   _____

99. Do you deliver dependable results without supervision?   _____

100. Are you absolutely loyal to your organization?   _____

Total Points   _____

Your Percentage of Efficiency (Divide Above Sum by 10)   _____

The Next Step

Now note your points of strength and weakness. Cash in on your strong points; improve and strengthen your weak points. Such a searching self-analysis is the first step toward intelligent development of your personality.

Acknowledgment

This self-improvement tool was designed by B. Weirauch, Vice President, Sales, Orr Iron Company, Inc., Evansville, Indiana. It is based on many years of careful study and counseling with large and varied groups of salespeople.

Now that you have completed your self-analysis, let us look at an eighth grade examination given in Salina, Kansas, at the turn of the nineteenth century.

Read the examination, take it, and you will soon find out how much examinations have changed. Compare this with one taken today on the same subjects. Over the past many years it has been downgraded ("dumbed down") to an unbelievable level.

It's not your fault. Your parents and grandparents did not want this to happen, so why did it happen? Consider the following widely accepted causes:

1. A change in the needs of families since the end of WWII.

2. The advent of television in the 1940s and early 1950s.

3. A breakdown of morals across the country in both two-parent and single-parent homes.

4. Use of legal and illegal drugs, with younger and younger children becoming addicted as they emulate their parents.

5. An attitude of a devil-may-care life: "Let the other guy fend for himself but not in my backyard."

6. One-person heads of households with "children having children."

7. Our social (political) system giving the government more *largess* to distribute with little or no accountability, giving economic pressures as the reason.

8. Political correctness. A virtual breakdown in the field of logic.

The above are just a few of the reasons our children cannot compete with children of many other countries where family discipline rules.

My question to you who now face the future is, what do you and your peers plan to do about the above?

1895 Eighth Grade Final Exam

Remember when our grandparents and great-grandparents stated that they only had an eighth-grade education? Well, check this out.

Could any of us have passed the eighth grade in 1895? This is the eighth grade final exam from 1895 in Salina, Kansas. It was taken from the original document on file at the Smokey Valley Genealogical Society and Library in Salina, Kansas, and reprinted by the *Salina Journal*.

Grammar (Time: One Hour)

1. Give nine rules for the use of capital letters.

2. Name the parts of speech and define those that have no modifications.

3. Define verse, stanza, and paragraph.

4. What are the principal parts of a verb? Give the principal parts of lie, lay, and run.

5. Define case; illustrate each case.

6. What is punctuation? Give rules for principal marks of punctuation.

7. Write a composition of about 150 words and show therein that you understand the practical use of the rules of grammar.

Arithmetic (Time: 1.25 Hours)

1. Name and define the fundamental rules of arithmetic.

2. A wagon box is 2 ft. deep, 10 ft. long, and 3 ft. wide. How many bushels of wheat will it hold?

3. If a load of wheat weighs 3942 lbs., what is it worth at 50 cts/bushel, deducting 1050 lbs. for tare?

4. District No. 33 has a valuation of $35,000. What is the necessary levy to carry on a school seven months at $50 per month and have $104 for incidentals?

5. Find the cost of 6720 lbs. of coal at $6.00 per ton.

6. Find the interest of $512.60 for 8 months and 18 days at 7 percent.

7. What is the cost of 40 boards 12 inches wide and 16 ft. long at $20 per meter?

8. Find bank discount on $300 for 90 days (no grace) at 10 percent.

9. What is the cost of a square farm at $15 per acre, the distance around which is 640 rods?

10. Write a bank check, promissory note, and a receipt.

US History (Time: 45 Minutes)

1. Give the epochs into which US history is divided.

2. Give an account of the discovery of America by Columbus.

3. Relate the causes and results of the Revolutionary War.

4. Show the territorial growth of the United States.

5. Tell what you can of the history of Kansas.

6. Describe three of the most prominent battles of the Rebellion.

7. Who were the following: Morse, Whitney, Fulton, Bell, Lincoln, Penn, and Howe?

8. Name events connected with the following dates: 1607, 1620, 1800, 1849, and 1865.

Orthography (Time: 1 Hour)

1. What is meant by the following: alphabet, phonetic, orthography, etymology, syllabification?

2. What are elementary sounds? How are they classified?

3. Explain each of the following and include an example of each: tri-graph, sub vocals, diphthong, cognate letters, linguals?

4. Give four substitutes for caret "u."

5. Give two rules for spelling words with final "e." Name two exceptions under each rule.

6. Give two uses of silent letters in spelling. Illustrate each.

7. Define the following prefixes and use in connection with a word: bi-, dis-, mis-, pre-, semi-, post-, non-, inter-, mono-, sup-.

8. Mark diacritically and divide into syllables the following, and name the sign that indicates the sound: card, ball, mercy, sir, odd, cell, rise, blood, fare, last.

9. Use the following correctly in sentences: cite, site, sight, fane, fain, feign, vane, vain, vein, raze, raise, rays.

10. Write 10 words frequently mispronounced and indicate pronunciation by use of diacritical marks and by syllabification.

Geography (Time: 1 Hour)

1. What is climate? Upon what does climate depend?

2. How do you account for the extremes of climate in Kansas?

3. Of what use are rivers? Of what use is the ocean?

4. Describe the mountains of North America.

5. Name and describe the following: Monrovia, Odessa, Denver, Manitoba, Hecla, Yukon, St. Helena, Juan Fernandez, Aspinwall, and Orinoco.

6. Name and locate the principal trade centers of the United States.

7. Name all the republics of Europe and give the capital of each.

8. Why is the Atlantic Coast colder than the Pacific in the same latitude?

9. Describe the process by which the water of the ocean returns to the sources of rivers.

10. Describe the movements of the earth. Give the inclination of the earth.

Also notice that the exam took five hours to complete. Gives the saying "She/he had only an 8th grade education" a whole new meaning, doesn't it? What happened to us? I didn't even understand some of the questions, let alone know all the answers!

On a More Serious Note

This test consists of one multiple-choice question (so you better get it right!). Here's a list compiled by historian William Blum of the countries that the US has bombed since the end of World War II:

China 1945–46

Korea 1950–53

China 1950–53

Guatemala 1954

Indonesia 1958

Cuba 1959–60

Guatemala 1960

Congo 1964

Peru 1965

Laos 1964–73

Vietnam 1961–73

Cambodia 1969–70

Guatemala 1967–69

Grenada 1983

Libya 1986

El Salvador 1980s

Nicaragua 1980s

Panama 1989

Iraq 1991–99; 2001–2009

Sudan 1998

Afghanistan 1998; 2001–2009

Yugoslavia 1999

In how many of these instances did a democratic government, respectful of human rights, occur as a direct result? Choose one of the following:

(a) 0

(b) Zero

(c) None

(d) Not a one

(e) Zip

(f) A whole number between -1 and + 1

(g) Zilch

The above test was included to remind you that we who live in the US have much to be thankful for. Most of us do live the "good life." If you feel you do not have it, just look in the mirror and ask yourself why. What are your reasons for not joining the majority of Americans who do enjoy the happy and comfortable life? We live in the greatest country in the whole world, having luxuries that were only an opportunity. Step up and be a part of it!

As you go from grade school to high school, you begin to mature both mentally and physically. As you advance in school, academics, athletics, and social activities, you begin to realize you are trusted with more responsibilities. When you reach the magic age of transition, you know that within a year or two you will graduate from high school and will be sent out to seek your dreams. So now you are really "growing up," whatever that means. And slowly but almost certainly, you make plans for your future. Is it a college nearby or someplace far from home, or do you plan to stay at home and get a job nearby? If you pick "going to college," many questions arise.

Money, an almost universal problem, no doubt heads the list. Close by is career. Are you firm in a decision to follow your dreams and have already picked your vocation, or do you plan to start college with general ideas of what you want to do in your lifetime and give yourself time to grow into the decision-making phase of your life?

Surely you have all read of the difference in earning power between those who graduate from college and those who are satisfied for whatever reason to complete high school and look for work.

With the above caveats in mind, do you have a life compass? Do you have any idea what you want to do with the rest of your life? Throughout this book we will give you many options and hints on how to accomplish your dreams. But there is one certain rule we must all live by: There is no free lunch.

Whatever career path you choose to pursue will have an impact on your future. Thus, we suggest you give full and ample thought to this very important time in your life. *Tempus fugit* ("Time flies").

Tomorrow You Will Graduate

ARE YOU READY?

Knowledge Is Energy for the Mind

In high school, my fellow students and I would ask, "Why do I have to do this?" or "I don't plan to go to Europe, so why do I have to study about it?" The answer our teachers gave was usually, "You might just need this knowledge in the future." (Little did we know World War II was just around the corner and that most all of us would be in it.) Maybe the teachers' words weren't too believable at the time, but nevertheless theirs was good advice. Example: Those of us who were proficient at math or science for the most part advanced more rapidly once America entered the war.

When I was a student in high school, I would hear other students say, "I cannot understand it," or "It is too complicated for me," and similar statements.

My reply to these statements was, "I have a friend who was blind from birth, raised a family, conquered learning the computer, and helped me teach a computer class. Not only is she good at what she does, but she is always friendly, a delightful conversationalist, and a constant learner regardless of the subject."

I have one question for you, "Could you do the same?"

So, when you go out to seek your fortune, just remember, it isn't easy.

A little knowledge will never hurt you, but a great deal of knowledge will probably set you above your peers.

Twenty-Five Things You Will Need to Know after High School

1. Don't sweat the small stuff, and remember, most stuff is small.

2. The most boring word in any language is "I."

3. Nobody is indispensable, especially you.

4. Life is full of surprises. Just say "never," and you'll see.

5. People are more important than things.

6. Persistence will get you almost anything eventually.

7. Nobody can make you happy. Most folks are about as happy as they make up their minds to be.

8. There's so much bad in the best of us and so much good in the worst of us that it doesn't behoove any of us to talk about the rest of us.

9. Live by what you trust, not by what you fear.

10. Character counts. Family matters.

11. Eating out with small children isn't worth it, even if someone else is buying.

12. If you wait to have kids until you can afford them, you probably never will.

13. Kittens don't begin to open their eyes for six weeks after birth. Humans generally take about twenty-six years.

14. The world would run a lot smoother if more men knew how to dance.

15. Television ruins more minds than do drugs.

16. Sometimes there is more to gain in being wrong than right.

17. Life is so much simpler when you tell the truth.

18. People who do the world's real work don't usually wear neckties.

19. A good joke beats a pill for a lot of ailments.

20. There are no substitutes for fresh air, sunshine, and exercise.

21. A smile is the cheapest way to improve your looks, even if your teeth are crooked.

22. May you live life so there is standing room only at your funeral.

23. Mothers always know best, but sometimes fathers know, too.

24. Forgive yourself, your friends, and your enemies. You're all only human.

25. If you don't do anything else in life, love someone and let someone love you.

—Author Unknown

Graduation Day

Finally the day has come; you have graduated from high school. Friends and relatives attend your graduation ceremonies, but what is your next move? If you plan to go to college in the fall, you start immediately to prepare for entrance into the new world. How do you do this? Read at least one book every week over the next ten or twelve weeks.

The books you read should be in the field of work you plan to study. You say you are not sure at this time of the program you want to study. Fine, read books about history, English, mathematics, and any subjects you know you will need in the future. In this manner, you can get a slight jump on your competition, which I assure you will be tough and tenacious.

And for those of you who do not plan to go to college or trade school, why not read and savor the joys of learning. Speaking from my eighty-seven years, I can say unequivocally that I have regretted the rest of my years after high school that I didn't read more and more often. Although I have had success as a businessman, I have a thirst for learning more and more regardless of the subject.

It is estimated that the difference between the earning potential of a high school diploma and a bachelor's degree is more than one million dollars over a lifetime.*

Found on the Internet

To anyone with kids of any age, here's some advice. It's a speech given at a high school about eleven things students will not learn in school. It addresses how feel-good, politically correct teachings have created a generation of kids with no concept of reality and how that sets them up for failure in the real world.

Rule 1: Life is not fair—get used to it!

Rule 2: The world won't care about your self-esteem. The world will expect you to accomplish something BEFORE you feel good about yourself.

Rule 3: You will NOT make $60,000 a year right out of high school. You won't be a vice-president with a car phone until you earn both.

Rule 4: If you think your teacher is tough, wait till you get a boss.

Rule 5: Flipping burgers is not beneath your dignity. Your grandparents had a different word for burger flipping: they called it opportunity.

---

*US Census Bureau, 2003

Rule 6: If you mess up, it's not your parents' fault, so don't whine about your mistakes; learn from them.

Rule 7: Before you were born, your parents weren't as boring as they are now. They got that way from paying bills, cleaning your clothes, and listening to you talk about how cool you thought you were. So before you save the rain forest from the parasites of your parents' generation, try delousing the closet in your own room.

Rule 8: Your school may have done away with winners and losers, but life HAS NOT. In some schools, they have abolished failing grades and they'll give you as MANY TIMES as you want to get the right answer. This doesn't bear the slightest resemblance to ANYTHING in real life.

Rule 9: Life is not divided into semesters. You don't get summers off, and very few employers are interested in helping you FIND YOURSELF. Do that on your own time.

Rule 10: Television is NOT real life. In real life people actually have to leave the coffee shop and go to jobs.

Rule 11: Be nice to nerds. Chances are you'll be working for one.

—Author Unknown

Signs of the Times

The following article was written in the year 2000:

Those of you born after 1982 can use this as a benchmark. If you do not recognize many of the statements here, then ask someone much older than you about them. You might find they, too, are outdated. The people who started college in 2006 across the nation were born in 1988.

- They have no meaningful recollection of the Reagan Era and probably did not know he had ever been shot.
- They were prepubescent when the Persian Gulf War was waged.
- Black Monday 1987 is as significant to them as the Great Depression.
- There has been only one Pope.
- They were 11 when the Soviet Union broke apart and do not remember the Cold War.
- They have never feared a nuclear war.

- They are too young to remember the space shuttle blowing up.
- Tiananmen Square means nothing to them.
- Their lifetime has always included AIDS.
- Bottle caps have always been screw-off and plastic.
- Atari predates them as do vinyl albums. The expression "you sound like a broken record" means nothing to them.
- They have never owned a record player.
- They have likely never played Pac-Man and have never heard of Pong.
- They may have never heard of an 8-track. The compact disc was introduced when they were five years old.
- As far as they know, stamps have always cost about 40–45 cents.
- They have always had a telephone answering machine.
- Most have never seen a TV set with only 13 channels, nor have they seen a black-and-white TV.
- They have always had cable.
- There have always been VCRs, but they have no idea what Beta is.
- They cannot fathom not having a remote control.
- They were born the year that Walkman® was introduced by Sony.
- Roller skating has always meant inline for them.
- Jay Leno has always been on *The Tonight Show*.
- They have no idea when or why Jordache jeans were cool.
- Popcorn has always been cooked in the microwave.
- They have never seen Larry Bird play basketball.
- They never took a swim and thought about *Jaws*.
- The Vietnam War is as ancient history to them as WWI, WWII, and the Civil War.
- They have no idea that Americans were ever held hostage in Iran.
- They can't imagine what hard contact lenses are.
- They don't know who Mork was or where he was from.
- They never heard: "Where's the beef?" "I'd walk a mile for a Camel," or "De plane, de plane!"
- They do not care who shot J.R. and have no idea who J.R. is.
- The *Titanic* was found? They thought we always knew where it was.
- Kansas, Chicago, Boston, America, and Alabama are places, not groups.
- McDonald's never came in Styrofoam containers.

- There has always been MTV.
- They don't have a clue how to use a typewriter.

We senior citizens do not expect you to know most of the above, but we can assure you that a good course in modern history may just fill you in on how fast your world is moving.

—Author Unknown

The Day after Graduation

ATTITUDE   ATTITUDE   ATTITUDE

"Attitude": The word is a noun, a thing that delights or attracts people. A bad attitude works in an opposite way of a good attitude. So let's get positive and go out and apply for a job. Good idea—but where do you go?

Check the want ads in the newspaper. Ask your friends if they know of any companies that are hiring. Prepare a resume. Try to include any and all skills you may have—e.g., if you took typing in school, how fast can you now type? Note: If your answer is less than sixty words per minute, I strongly urge you to keep practicing and reach at least eighty! Once you do so, your odds of being hired will greatly improve.

Let's assume you are called in for an interview, are hired, and start work the following Monday. Naturally, you should dress appropriately for the job: work clothes for ordinary labor and dress clothes for office work. Smile when you enter the office or factory. Introduce yourself to your peers, and ask for their help if you need it. Work hard, as if your life depended on it. You will soon discover whether you like your job, and your boss will learn whether he or she likes you. This is all-important. Many persons are hired on a ninety-day trial period. After that testing period, you will probably know enough about the job to wish to stay or leave, and, likewise, your boss will know whether he or she wants to retain you. It is always nice if you are lucky on your first job, but, if you are not, there are other jobs and other places.

As an example of being in the right place at the right time, consider this true story from my own life. A few days after Pearl Harbor in December 1941, which was the start of America's involvement in WWII, a group of my fellow students and I walked (none of us had cars) to downtown Oshkosh, Wisconsin, and enlisted in the Air Force.

As luck would have it, so many young Americans signed up for the service that we were not called for duty until June of 1942. Sworn in by an Army major in Milwaukee, we were taken by train to Lackland Air Force Base near San Antonio, Texas. After basic training, we were shipped to Cimarron Field, near Oklahoma City, Oklahoma, to take primary training. About six weeks later, I flunked out due to air sickness and was sent to Vance Air Base in Enid, Oklahoma, to work on basic flight aircraft (the second phase of flying). At that time we were asked by the sergeant in charge which job we would like to do: work as a mechanic in the hanger or outside on the line. I did not volunteer for either job but asked to work in the office. The sergeant said, "Okay, go into the office and ask for M/Sgt. Young," which I did and was welcomed. He was about forty years old, sunburned, and bald. He had been transferred from the Cavalry to the Air Force, and I thought he was the oldest man in the world.

About a week later the phone rang. M/Sgt. Young answered and, upon completion of the call, turned to me and said, "We are starting a new air base in Kansas." My immediate reaction was, "May I go with you?" His answer was, "That is a good idea." A few days later, twenty-five young airmen got off the bus, and M/Sgt. Young, whose home was Atoka, Oklahoma, said, "You are all staff sergeants." Imagine our surprise and happiness—a jump in rank from private to staff sergeant in one fell swoop—more money, more prestige, and more responsibility.

The moral of this story is "Ask and you shall receive," and you could be there too.

Another story about much greater success concerns a child, born in poverty and without a father, who went to school where his peers called him a "dummy."

His mother, though completely without education, took her two boys to the library and asked the librarian to give both of them two books each week to read. Sometime later, when a school superintendent walked into the classroom and asked the class about some rocks, this child was the only one to respond with the answer. Everyone was amazed when this "dummy" was asked how he knew the answer and he replied, "I read it in a book." From that time on, he was at the head of his class, went on to high school, then to college, and eventually became a world-renowned surgeon at Johns Hopkins Hospital in Baltimore. His name is Dr. Ben Carson. You see, it can be done.

OPPORTUNITY   OPPORTUNITY   OPPORTUNITY

One could write a book on the thousands and thousands of success stories. Many would be about good luck, but many more would be about hard work. There is a story that there were two knocks at the door of a house, and a voice from within said, "Who is it?" The person outside said, "*Opportunity*." The answer from the inside came back, "No, it isn't; '*opportunity*' only knocks once." This aphorism is very good to remember. Stay awake and watch for new job opportunities, new promotions, and upward changes in management. No position is static forever. If businesses do not move up with the times, they are almost certain to fail. Why should you be any different?

What happened to the "horse and buggy" many years ago? What happened to the Model T Ford? What happened to the typewriter? What happened to the old "ice box"? They all have one thing in common: They were "done in" as our friends, the British, would say.

Today you graduates can look forward to thousands of new inventions, progress in the fields of medicine, electronics, science, photography, and so on. Where will you be as these changes occur?

It is strictly up to you. Do you want to join the team of progress, or will you be satisfied to get a mediocre job with low or mediocre pay?

Although you may not have started on the right path, it is never too late to change.

The fact is that you can change your compass to guide you into the twenty-first century by completing this book, rechecking your attitude, becoming a better and happier person, and learning more throughout your life. You are young, you're pliable, and your whole life is in front of you. Don't let this opportunity pass you by!

Let us now move on to the next chapter and learn how to sell.

After Graduation

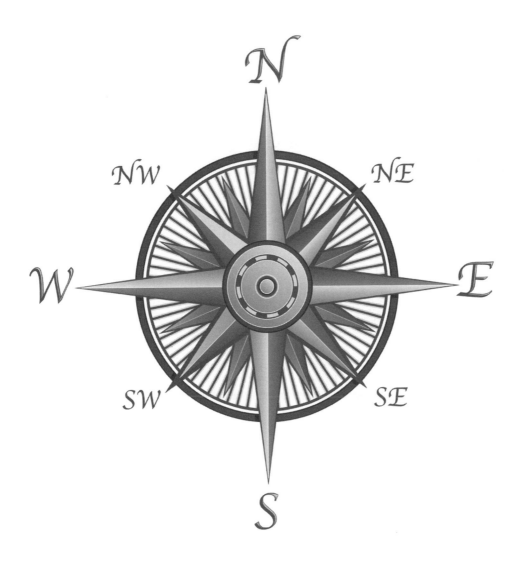

The Compass of Your Life

Which direction are you going?

In the field of selling the first thing to remember is, "You can never make a second first impression." The impression you make as you meet your prospective client hinges on your every move: how you walk, how you stand, how you smile, your first words. You need to consider all of the following:

- Start at the top. Do you have a fresh haircut or hairdo?
- Are you well shaved or pleasantly made up?
- Are your teeth brushed and is your breath fresh?
- Is your suit or dress clean and fresh?
- What about your shirt and undergarments?
- Are your nails clipped and manicured?
- Is your belt clean and matching your outer garments?
- Do your socks match your clothes?
- Do your shoes match your outer garments, and are they polished?
- Don't chew gum.
- Never, ever smoke during a sales call even if your prospect does.
- Remember that listening is equal to or more important than talking.
- Keep up your enthusiasm and smile as if you've already made the sale.

Chapter 2
Selling

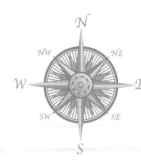

What Is Selling?

SIMPLY PUT, IT is one individual persuading one or more other persons to purchase or use a product. It matters not whether your product is tangible or intangible.

Approach a sale by doing the following:

1. Organizing your thoughts on "How to"

2. Learning as much as you can about your product or service

3. Using selling aids, i.e., actual products, pictures, articulating a verbal explanation of what, where, when, why, and how

4. Finding out the customer's needs

5. Filling the customer's needs

6. Overcoming objections

7. Pointing out features

8. Showing benefits

9. Speaking like a professional and articulating the benefits

10. Focusing on the buyer, not the observer

11. Recognizing objections and when and how to handle them

12. Summarizing and restating any objections and demonstrating the logic of overcoming them

13. Following the objections and restating all necessary selling points

14. Exuding confidence at all times

15. Going home with a sale

Continuing Sales Education

In 1951 this author enrolled in a sales course conducted by the Elmer Wheeler Sales Institute in South Bend, Indiana. Wheeler was author of many books and also many one-liners. Probably his most famous one was "Don't sell the steak; sell the sizzle." Another is "Boy, am I enthusiastic." I still awaken every morning and repeat the latter ten times. It puts me in a happy frame of mind, eager to start the day. It seems to me I wake up Monday morning, and it is already Friday afternoon.

There are literally hundreds of books about salesmanship in the marketplace. Browse your library and take a couple of books home with you. They are usually fun to read, always educational, and you may pick up new ideas to help you in your job, marriage, or among friends. Another point Elmer taught was, "Don't ask if; ask which." In other words, always give the other person a choice between two things they want.

Enthusiasm breeds more enthusiasm. It is a part of being happy. It brings smiles and happiness to those around us.

Other one-liners we learned were:

- "The heart is closer to the pocketbook than the brain."
- "Always assume you are going to get the order."
- "A sale is an agreement, not an argument."
- "Plan your sales talk from the prospect's point of view."
- "One minute of demonstration takes the place of one hour of conversation."

Probably more sales have been lost because of overselling (talking too much) than not talking enough.

Notes on Sales and Salesmanship

Be on time always.

As you discuss your product with a prospect, point out the features, then pick up the product, place it on the floor so it will not distract the prospect, and proceed to tell him or her of the benefits.

Five Important Steps

1. Give undivided attention to your prospect.

2. Show the prospect the advantage.

3. Prove the advantage.

4. Persuade the prospect to grasp it.

5. Ask for the order.

Remember, a sale is made on every call; either you sell the prospect(s), or they sell you.

Don't sell your product or service; sell the result it will produce.

Close as soon as you can and as often as you can. Keep asking for the order.

If an account is lost, find out the reason. You can always go back to ask the client why he or she stopped doing business with you. This gives you another chance to resell him or her later.

The Joys of Selling

One of the joys of selling is the opportunity to meet many different types of people. The nature of the product you are selling can limit the scope and area in which you are able to operate. For example, if you are selling hearing aids, normally your clientele would be the elderly. If you are selling services, such as repairing computers, you are likely to be limited to the area where your business is located.

Thus, when you decide to get into selling, think of the travel you may encounter, the cost you may incur without reimbursement, and so on. Ask a mentor (or mentors) for advice about starting a business venture and about some of the pitfalls you may encounter. Unless they are of a different breed, we say, "Never go into business where you must work nights or Sundays." We also say, "Never go into a business where you have to wait for business to come to you. Be able to go out and ask for it to come to you." Again, there are exceptions to this rule.

Most of my adult life was spent in the computer business. Starting in 1951, I purchased a franchise from the Accounting Corp. of America of San Diego, California. I chose St. Joseph County in South Bend, Indiana, for a home office.

A couple of years later I purchased the franchise for the entire state of Indiana as my exclusive territory for selling our services to certified public accountants and public accountants. This arrangement meant some travel, some overnight. My objective was to sign up as many accounting firms as I could because I would receive a $1.00 royalty for each business account processed by our home office.

The fun part came in many venues—meeting intelligent people, having lunch with business people who basically had the same problems, visiting interesting places like museums, fine restaurants, historical buildings, and so on. My clientele shared many of my interests and seemed to vie for my friendship for various reasons—one was tickets for a Notre Dame football game. So with the building of friendships between our families, we traveled across the good old USA and once, for study and recreation, to Spain.

Col. Harland Sanders

Among the interesting persons I met during my years in selling was Col. Harland Sanders, famous around the world for his "finger-lickin' good" chicken. One of the Colonel's franchise holders introduced me to this great entrepreneur who started his business in Shelbyville, Kentucky, after he reached the magic age of sixty-five. He had previously been in business in Corbin, Kentucky, owning a motel and restaurant near the Tennessee border. When our various states started connecting federal highways, Corbin was bypassed by Highway 75, which traversed mid-America from northern Michigan to southern Florida. This change caused the Colonel to give up his business location and start a whole new venture of franchising. His timing could not have been better. The word "franchising" was relatively new in the business world. With changes in eating habits, however, food franchises became household names. One of the leaders was Kentucky Fried Chicken (KFC).

The knowledge that the Colonel had obtained over the years proved invaluable to his quest for success in promoting his expertise in cooking and marketing fried chicken. Starting out in an old Cadillac, with boxes of pots and pans, the Colonel would stop at the first restaurant he would come to and ask whether he could cook the dinner for them that day. Some said "Yes" whereas others said "No." The restaurant owners were not only impressed by the taste of the chicken (a secret recipe developed by the Colonel) but also his showmanship in presenting his product. He was a handsome man dressed in a white suit and shirt along with black shoes and a black tie. He would visit the diners eating his gourmet food and explain his cooking process.

Customers were impressed, and before long the Colonel could set you up as a franchise holder and show you how to make a good living cooking chicken. Here was the ideal "first impression," as no matter where the Colonel traveled, heads turned when he walked by, be it in an airport, service station, or another restaurant.

The Colonel didn't drink or smoke but would cough and sputter if someone smoked nearby. His franchised outlets were to be meticulously clean, and he had company representatives stop in unexpectedly to assure they stayed that way. Woe be to the violator who didn't obey the standards of cleanliness. I had the pleasure of living in the Colonel's beautiful country home in Shelbyville, Kentucky, about twenty-five miles from Louisville, Kentucky. After work, the Colonel and his wife Claudia and I would visit a local eatery (no, it didn't have to be a KFC restaurant), and we would discuss our future together. He was a delightful straight shooter, always fair, and a pleasure to be with. A few years after his seventy-fifth birthday party, the Colonel decided it was time to sell his business. He did so with the same class as he did everything else.

Dave Thomas

Dave Thomas started out in life as an orphan but, as a young boy, found two brothers in Fort Wayne, Indiana, willing to give him a job in their restaurant (later to become a KFC franchise). From Fort Wayne, Dave was named manager of five KFC locations in Columbus, Ohio, where he turned a corporation that was losing money into a profit-making business before the end of his first year as manager. I had the pleasure of riding with Dave to Fort Wayne, Indiana, where we consummated a business deal with his ex-bosses. Dave went on to be a TV star for his own company, Wendy's. Dave started this new franchise after he had sold his stock in the company that had bought out the Colonel. This time it was hamburgers. Laid back, quiet, and unassuming, Dave, along with some savvy businessmen, made it big—really big—in the franchise world. My wife owns stock in the company and is well pleased with the results.

Dave, a completely different sales type from the Colonel, had all the basic ingredients to become an entrepreneur. He was intelligent, modest, hardworking, honest, and friendly. The rest of the Wendy's story is yet to be told. Dave died a few years ago, but his company is still growing and continues to be one of the premier franchises in the USA and around the world.

Astronaut John L. (Jack) Swigert

Jack Swigert, with a little luck at being in the right place at the right time, became command pilot of Apollo 13. Heading for the moon, the crew heard an explosion behind the space they were occupying. Some of you reading about this most phenomenal story may not know the details of how the three survived the explosion while on their way to land on the moon, although others may have seen Ron Howard's film *Apollo 13*, which is supposedly a quite accurate recreation of these events.

The astronauts assessed the damage to their spacecraft as best they could, relayed messages back to earth, and attempted to coordinate their flight with a dwindling supply of oxygen while trying to follow suggestions from Houston on how they could return safely to earth. After circling the moon, they pointed their Apollo toward earth.

In the meantime, Base Houston had everyone available calculating distances with slide rules since there were no computers fast enough to fulfill their needs. With duct tape and a cardboard box, the crew was able to distribute enough oxygen to stay alive even though temperatures were approaching freezing.

Finally, after many hours of anxiety, the crew re-entered the earth's atmosphere and landed on the Pacific Ocean safe and sound—certainly one of the miracles of the day.

My purpose in telling you the stories of these three men is that I knew them all and that any of you could have been them. Sound preposterous? Not really. None of those three in their wildest dreams in their younger days could have realized their contributions to the US. Note that Jack came home to Denver, ran for Congress from the Denver area, and won the election but never served a day in Congress. He died before he took office.

Thus, as time marches on, I have lost three good friends.

Steps to Avoid Failure

1. Don't be too dependent on your "good" accounts. Tomorrow they could swear allegiance to someone else.

2. Don't forget to sell the strengths of your company; your competitors are selling their strengths.

3. "I can save you money" is a strong statement for a salesperson to make. "I can help you make more money" is a stronger one and puts the seller into a counseling position rather than a competitive one.

4. Don't forget that someone will always have a lower price—that means you need something more than price to sell.

5. You can never do too much research. You can never have too much information. The trick is to organize the knowledge you have and use it when needed.

6. Treat small accounts with respect, understanding, and the expectation that they'll soon be big accounts.

7. Try to promise a little more than you can deliver and always deliver a little more than you promise. In other words, to stand out from the crowd, stretch yourself and your capabilities.

Sales Demonstration Checklist

Ask yourself:

- Is the demonstration needed and appropriate?
- Have I developed a specific demonstration objective?
- Have I properly planned and organized the demonstration?
- Have I rehearsed to the point that the demonstration flows smoothly and appears to be natural?
- What is the probability the demonstration will go as planned?
- What is the probability the demonstration will backfire?
- Does my demonstration present my product in an ethical and professional manner?

Toastmasters

Salesmanship, like any occupation, requires continuing education. One of the best ways to upgrade your selling skills is to join Toastmasters. When you join, you will learn how to speak, be it for one, two, or five minutes. You will also learn how to critique the speaker(s), all in good friendship and all for your betterment. Easy to join, with very little cost, Toastmasters usually meets once a week, with up to thirty members per chapter.

We are talking about being a salesperson selling a product. We are talking about becoming a better communicator with almost everyone and improving your vocabulary. You will learn how to smile more often, stand erect, dress properly, and get rid of annoying habits you may not have known you had. You will also cultivate new friends. Given the investment in terms of time and money, it will certainly be worthwhile.

Another means of self-improvement is to take a Dale Carnegie course. Similar to Toastmasters, Carnegie offers most of the same suggestions that can improve your whole outlook on life.

Check out your phone directory or chamber of commerce to find Dale Carnegie courses or Toastmasters.

What's in a Name?

The word a person likes to hear more than any other word is his or her name.

Roll call at 6:00 A.M. in the Air Force was a daily ritual. The 1ˢᵗ Sgt or the orderly clerk had the honor of yelling out the airman's last name, and that person had better answer, no matter how his name was barbecued. If he didn't respond because he wasn't in the lineup, rest assured he had better have a good reason for not being there, or he could quickly find himself on the way to the guard house (that's jail, for the uninformed).

As you are introduced to another person, look him or her straight in the eye and, if you didn't hear the person's name, ask him or her to repeat it. When you are doing the introduction, it is easy to spell the person's last name, and it will be much easier for the person being introduced to remember. Example: "Matt Ferris, I would like to have you meet a friend of mine, Rick Ballew, spelled B-a-l-l-e-w, easy to say and easy to remember."

So if someone asks you, "What's in a name?" you can say, "Everything."

People love to hear their names mentioned.

Credit is due to my brother-in-law, John Brademas, former Congressman from Indiana, for this way of making an introduction.

Having a Hard Time Finding a Job?

Consider the following:

What do you have to offer an employer? If you have no skills or the minimum thereof, have you thought of attending a night school to increase your knowledge on specific or general subjects? English or mathematics should be your first as they will be needed for the rest of your life.

Have you looked in a mirror and asked yourself, "What do I really want to do in life? Am I qualified to do it?"

Do you have a good and proper attitude? Are you willing to take almost any job to start? If not, why not?

Is earning money the only reason you want a job? If your answer is yes, please read Chapter 6, because there are other things besides money.

Are you willing to take a part-time job regardless of the amount of pay and bad hours to get a start? If not, why not?

Do you feel the government owes you a living today, next month, next year? If your answer is yes to all, you really should get help on your attitude.

Are you aware of the cost an employer has to bear over and above your salary? It is in excess of 25 percent of your gross earnings.

Example: If you are earning $8.00 per hour, just add another $2.00 per hour for the employer's expense.

Add training time to the above. I haven't researched the cost today, but, about fifty years ago, the Indiana Restaurant Association calculated the cost of training a waitress was over $1,000.00. The only way to find out is to go into business for yourself, and you will soon agree, it isn't easy for the boss or the employee.

The Interview

If you have a job interview, try to make it as pleasant as possible.

After you receive a call from a business wishing to interview you, research the company as to the type, size, number of employees, and any other pertinent information that may be helpful to you.

I recently talked to a man who had just finished college, answered an ad, was called in for an interview, and out of twenty-one applicants was the only one to have knowledge about the company doing the interviewing. He was hired and is now moving up the ladder of success.

During the interview he was asked how he knew so much about the company. His answer: "Well, if I am going to work for this company, I thought I should learn as much as I could about it in advance." He also said, "It made my interview very simple and rewarding."

There are other ways to learn about a company, such as asking your banker or other business people what they know about it. You may even get a reference from them if they are close to any of the senior employees. You may find that a close neighbor works for the company and will give you the name of the hiring agent. You may be pleasantly surprised by getting the position you seek because someone put in a kind word for you.

But we are ahead of ourselves. First we must follow the advice of thousands, and, yes, millions of people who have gone before you. They paid their dues, so to speak. They also offer you experience accumulated over a lifetime. Take advantage of it and don't abuse it.

If you get a job, you've consummated a sale: You've sold the employer on hiring you. In essence, though, two sales, not one, will have been made because the boss will have sold you on coming to work for the company.

Here's an example of how someone can get hired: A man took his grandson to an interview for a job that was open for a truck driver's position. Before the interview, the grandfather had a chance to talk briefly with the business owner.

A couple of days later the grandson was hired. A couple of months went by and all was going well at the Whims and Wishes furniture store and a conversation broke out about various store issues. During this exchange of ideas, the owner told the grandson the reason he hired him was that he had a chauffeur's driver's license and that his grandfather had brought him into the store for the interview. The point being—you often don't know at the time what, exactly, will land you a position.

After making a cold call on a businessman in the computer business in West Palm Beach, Florida, I had the opportunity to ask him what I had said that made him join our company's service bureau. He smiled and said, "If the company I joined was indicative of the quality of employee who called on me, I wanted to do business with them."

Moral of the above: Pick your words carefully when you are attempting to make a sale, regardless of who the recipient may be.

An old expression says that if you goof up and say something insulting to someone, "It is better to eat crow while it is still warm, and it is easier to swallow, and it tastes better that way."

Making Cold Calls

Making cold calls can be a most enjoyable experience. During your calls, you teach, you learn, you practice, and if you do it right, you can make more money than you ever thought possible.

How can this be, you ask? It is quite simple if you follow the rules of selling. There are many ways of handling objections. One quick way is to ask a question of your prospect. Example: "Have I explained this to your satisfaction?" That will get the prospect talking and give you a chance to collect your sales talk ideas and take a different approach to clarify your points and set his or her mind at ease.

While living in Chicago and working for the Accounting Corp. of America, a national computer service bureau, I had the luxury of having the downtown area as my territory. This meant I was working in a heavy concentration of certified public accountants. There might be as many as fifteen or twenty firms in one building. What advantage would this be?

1. The most time I would lose in travel would be when a prospect wasn't in or was busy with a client, thus forcing me to make a second call at a later date. Should I be successful in making a sale, I could quickly ask if he knew of any other accountants in this building or nearby. Many times the answer was "yes" because of the fact that using our product saved him time and labor costs, and he was pleased to recommend me. Many times he would even call one or more of his associates and even set up appointments for me.

2. A stock-in-trade answer was, "He was too small," or "He didn't do write-up work," this being done by clerical staff. When I overcame his argument by showing him that he, too, could save time on the work he did, I ended up with another sale.

Don't misunderstand me—all sales were not that easy, so in one case I had to change my plan of attack. One of the CPA firms I visited employed a young lady who was evidently there to protect her boss. After four unsuccessful attempts to make an appointment with him, I finished my work for the day, went back to the office, and wrote a letter to this man whom I had never met. (I was able to get a business card before leaving the firm's waiting room.)

In the letter I explained the efforts I expended to make an appointment with him. Sending the letter marked personal and confidential, I awaited his reply. Three days later the phone rang. We set up an appointment for a time amenable for both of us, the sale was consummated, and I had a new client.

The cold, hard fact is that you are selling every day whether you have thought about it or not. You sell your partner on taking a vacation, on buying a new car, on changing your job. You sell young people on the rewards of education, of being honest and truthful at all times. You sell them on the importance of developing good relationships with their classmates.

What we are saying is sell, sell, sell.

The moral of the story is "Don't give up; try another angle. If the prospect has a need and you can fill that need, keep trying; the odds are in your favor."

Why Customers Quit

Reasons Customers Quit:

1% Die

3% Move away

5% Go to another friend in a similar business

9% Competitive reasons (e.g., price)

14% Product dissatisfaction

But...

68% Quit because of attitude of indifference toward customers by some employee

The Salesman

And in those days, behold, there came through the gates of the city a salesman from afar off, and it came to pass, as the day went by, he sold plenty.

And in that city were they that were the order takers and they that spent their days in adding to the alibi sheets. Mightily were they astonished? They said one to the other, "What the hell; how doth he get-eth away with it?" And it came to pass that many were gathered in the back office, and a soothsayer came among them. And he was one wise guy. And they spoke and questioned him saying, "How is it that this stranger accomplished the impossible?"

Whereupon the soothsayer made answer, "He of whom you speak is one hustler. He ariseth very early in the morning and goeth forth full of pep. He complaineth not, neither doth he know despair. He is arrayed in purple and fine linen, while ye go forth with pants unpressed.

"While ye gather here and say one to the other, 'Verily this is a terrible day to work', he is already abroad. And when the eleventh hour cometh, he needeth no alibis. He knoweth his line and they that would stave him off, give him orders. Men say unto him 'nay' when he cometh in, yet when he goeth forth he hath their names on the line that is dotted.

"He taketh with him the two angels, 'inspiration' and 'perspiration,' and worketh to beat hell. Verily I say unto you, go and do likewise."

—Author Unknown

Chapter 3

Personal Financial Planning

"It is far better to spend what is left after saving than to save what is left after spending."

—Benjamin Franklin

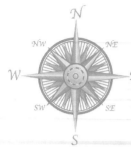

About Saving Money

NOTHING SHOULD MOTIVATE you more than having a nest egg for a financial emergency. Once you have reached this goal, you should develop a manageable plan to put money away where it is not readily available to spend but always there if and when you need it. If you see something you like—really like—think long and hard before you upset your plans to save for your future retirement. Just get into the habit of paying yourself first. You will never be sorry. So now read the next chapter on saving money.

On Savings

So much is written, but so little of it followed.

This chapter on saving money and time, if followed, could change your whole life for the better.

To prove a point, I challenge you to start today keeping a record of two things: the money you spend and the time you waste.

	Money spent	Time wasted
Day 1	_____	_____
Day 2	_____	_____
Day 3	_____	_____
...and on for an entire month		
Day 30	_____	_____
Totals	**Total money spent:** _____	**Total hours wasted:** _____

There is only one player in this game. After you analyze the month, you should come out the winner.

If you want a job well done, give it to a busy person.

Budget and Cash Flow

Every year-end—but anytime, like today—is a good time to set up a budget for the entire upcoming year. Then keep track of your income and expenses by using the budget form on the next page. The better you keep track of your income and expenses, the more you will realize how much money you waste. Learn how to stop the waste and invest the funds for your future.

This easy-to-read financial statement will help you get on the right path to financial security. The statement is easy to complete and requires only a few moments each month to accomplish.

PERSONAL ASSETS		PERSONAL LIABILITIES	
CASH	$ _____	CREDIT CARD(S)	$ _____
SAVINGS	$ _____	AUTO LOANS	$ _____
AUTOMOBILE	$ _____	STUDENT LOANS	$ _____
REAL ESTATE	$ _____	MORTGAGES	$ _____
		OTHER LOANS	$ _____
CASH VALUE OF LIFE INSURANCE	$ _____		
OTHER ASSETS	$ _____	OTHER LIABILITIES	$ _____
TOTAL PERSONAL ASSETS	$ _____		
TOTAL LIABILITIES	$ _____		
TOTAL NET WORTH (Assets minus liabilities) =	$ _____		

Use the following sheet to make blank copies as your finances change.

HOUSEHOLD CASH FLOW

Year: ☐

INCOME

	Jan	Feb	Mar	Apr	May	Jun	Jul	Aug	Sep	Oct	Nov	Dec	Year's Total
Wages/Salary 1													
Wages/Salary 2													
Interest & Dividends													

EXPENDITURES

	Jan	Feb	Mar	Apr	May	Jun	Jul	Aug	Sep	Oct	Nov	Dec	Year's Total
Mortgage/Rent													
Maintenance/Repairs													
Taxes													
Furniture/Appliances													
Auto Insurance													
Auto Keep up & Fuel													
Auto Loan/Lease Payment													
Credit Card/Other Loans													
Groceries & Other Food													
Health Care/Medical Costs													
Clothing													
School Expenses													
Child Care													
Utilities (Power, Heat, Etc.)													
Telephone & Cable TV													
Travel & Recreation													
Subscriptions/Memberships													
Charitable Contributions													
Other													

The previous pages allow you to get a bird's-eye view of where your money is going. Note: Some items are paid monthly and others periodically. Either way, you should (must) know your total expenses each and every month. Now, fill out a Cash Flow of Income and Expense sheet of the items you know (or can estimate) and label it #1, then divide by 30 to find out what it costs you to live each and every day. That very important information should spur you on to develop a savings plan. We'll have more on that later.

Now, take another Cash Flow of Income and Expense sheet and label it #2 and fill in all the items as you pay them: the utilities, clothing, recreation, etc. After a few short months you will quickly see what your expenses actually are (i.e., what it is costing you to live) and what you have left for savings or emergencies.

Stop right here.

In life there are only two givens, death and taxes, and that is the truth. Throughout life, there are good times and bad times. As you leave high school or college, the odds are that you have not yet suffered a great traumatic experience, but, by the age of forty years or thereabouts, it is almost certain you will lose a loved one. You may also witness a great war, an inflationary period (short or long), or a debilitating disease—all possible, plus old age without money. At least one of these is a certainty.

If you will follow the rules I am laying out for you, you will almost certainly eliminate one of the most important problems, i.e., being broke in your old age. Did you know that 95 percent of people living in the US are not wealthy? Are you going to be one of the 95 percent? You don't have to be. Start today. Set up the Cash Flow of Income and Expenses form and look for ways to reduce unnecessary expenditures. Example:

Eliminate your cell phone with an estimated cost of $50.00 per month or $600.00 per year. You say you cannot get along without it. Drop the cable with TV. You don't believe you can drop that either. Then reduce your vacation expenditures. Instead of eating lunch at a restaurant each day, try "brown bagging" it to work. You will find this change a great experience and a great money saver. Or, if you smoke, stop smoking. Buy a water filter for the water you carry with you. There are other ways to reduce expenses and save if you look closely at your expenditures, but first you must stop spending and start saving.

Take a good look at all your day's activities. You will surely find items you don't need or can do without. You can give up owning pets, which can be very expensive and interfere with saving for your future. Of course, though, the companionship is more than worth it for many people. You might consider giving up using ATMs, especially those from a bank different from your own that charge transaction fees. Or consider sharing an apartment until you can afford to be on your own. Use coupons when you shop at the grocery store. Make a list of things to buy and combine them into one trip, saving precious gas and precious time. Stop buying that expensive coffee. Is it really that much better tasting than what you brew at home? Use the Internet for shopping, to cut your monthly costs in half and come up with more ideas on saving.

Once you have cut back on your "really-do-not-need" items, take these savings, start investing them, and pledge to yourself you will not invade this nest egg unless it is for a serious emergency. Anyone can save for a rainy day, but having the fortitude to keep saving and adding to your savings is a whole new ballgame. As mentioned before, nine out of ten people who reach the age of sixty-five are not wealthy. Do you want to be in that group?

Plastic Money

Plastic money: What is it? How do you use it? When, why, and where?

Made of plastic, a little 2 x 3 inch credit card is a wonderful invention—if you use it properly. The word "if" really should be capitalized because of the credit card's powers to help and destroy you.

Some of the advantages of using a credit card are:

- It is small and easy to carry in your billfold.
- It can help you buy many things (maybe too many).
- It can be used as identification at airport rentals.
- It can be used in most financial emergencies, if you haven't maxed out the credit allowed you.
- If you pay on time (the date agreed on), there is no interest charge.
- You are able in most cases to get easy credit, even when a bank wouldn't consider giving you a small loan.

Some disadvantages of owning a credit card are:

- It makes it much too easy to borrow now and pay later.
- People need (or think they need) a given item and, before they realize it, end up deep in debt and forced to pay very high interest rates.
- Some states allow usurious rates of interest to be charged. (Any interest rate over 8 percent is usurious.)
- A late payment can mean a higher rate of interest on your balance.

Paying the credit card company a small monthly payment can stretch your obligation far into the future. Minimum monthly payments are expensive because of the high interest rates on most charge card balances.

NO FREE LUNCH!

We remind you there is no "free lunch."

Of all the caveats in life about "Don't do this or don't do that," think about the possibility of losing your job and finding yourself deep in debt with interest charges still continuing and most likely at a higher rate. A word to the wise should be sufficient.

More on Your Budget

When you buy a home and need a mortgage, you will also be required to have mortgage insurance. This should not be a problem, but my suggestion is that you take out a decreasing term life insurance (see Chapter 5).

This decision could save you about two-thirds the normal cost you would have incurred if you had purchased regular mortgage insurance.

This is also true when you finance an automobile. The sales person will offer you a package deal, which includes finance charges. He or she wants to sell you a vehicle of some type, and you are excited about driving off in a new or used car.

Now is the time to stop, take a deep breath, and review the contract presented to you. If you check only one item in this contract, it should be finance charges. You can quickly buy a term life insurance policy to cover the amount of your contract. Doing so will only delay your purchase a few hours but could save you many dollars. That money is just as good in your pocket as is in the car dealer's. Enough said.

You should also shop for the best interest rate because even half of 1 percent can make a sizeable difference in the amount you spend buying your home. Buying your home will probably be the greatest outlay of money you will make in your lifetime. Further recommendations are:

Finance your home over a ten-year period, and your interest will cost you one time your original cost. Finance your home for twenty years, and your cost is twice what you paid for it. Finance it for thirty years, and your cost will be three times the original price. Think of the savings you could make by sacrificing upfront and increasing your net worth and not paying the lending institution all that money over x number of years.

Ask your potential lender to provide you with amortization schedules showing payments for ten, twenty, and thirty years. Also ask for the interest rate quoted. It is only good business to shop for the best rate available to you. You will be glad you did.

If you take the difference in dollars plus one percent less or one percent higher than the price quoted, you may be shocked at the difference. What compensates for the pain of saving is the payoff from compounding interest.

This is a relatively straightforward mathematical process by which your money increases in value, slowly at first, then with much more dramatic speed. The following table illustrates the power of compounding interest for a saver who deposits $300 a month.

Compounding Table for Saver Depositing $300 a Month

After Tax Return	Year 5	Year 10	Year 15	Year 20	Year 25
4%	$19,890	$44,175	$ 73,827	$110,032	$154,239
5%	$20,402	$46,585	$ 80,187	$123,310	$178,653
6%	$20,931	$49,164	$ 87,246	$138,612	$207,898
7%	$21,478	$51,925	$ 95,089	$156,278	$243,022
8%	$22,043	$54,884	$103,811	$176,706	$285,308
9%	$22,627	$58,054	$113,522	$200,366	$336,337

Saving well means saving regularly and, ideally, early. That way your money has plenty of time to compound. For most people, this means having more than just the desire to save.

Setting up a Savings Plan

The key to building wealth successfully through savings is to have a plan. There are many ways to accomplish this goal, but here's a method that many people find useful.

Step 1: Start As Soon As Possible

Don't wait until some ideal time to start your savings plan. No time will seem ideal; you'll always find excuses to delay another month. At some point you simply have to take the plunge. The earlier you start, the better "grip" you'll have on your finances.

Step 2: Forecast Your Cash Flow

You should forecast your anticipated cash flow for various increments of the year. Usually this means forecasting the year on a monthly basis. Once you determine your income and expenses, how much is left over?

Step 3: Project Monthly Savings

Start with anticipated monthly savings, then project savings for the entire year. Doing so may involve averaging. For instance, if you can save $330 in February and $270 in March, you might decide to save $300 a month.

Ernst & Young's Personal Financial Planning Guide

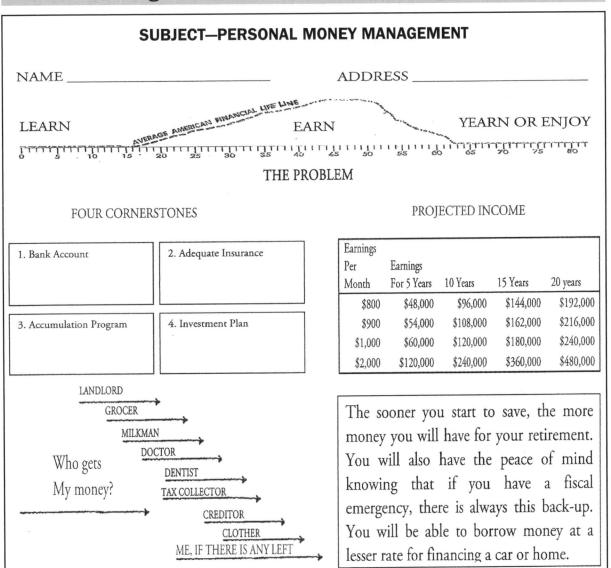

SUBJECT—PERSONAL MONEY MANAGEMENT

NAME _____   ADDRESS _____

LEARN   EARN   YEARN OR ENJOY

AVERAGE AMERICAN FINANCIAL LIFE LINE

0   5   10   15   20   25   30   35   40   45   50   55   60   65   70   75   80

THE PROBLEM

FOUR CORNERSTONES   PROJECTED INCOME

| 1. Bank Account | 2. Adequate Insurance |
| 3. Accumulation Program | 4. Investment Plan |

Earnings Per Month	Earnings For 5 Years	10 Years	15 Years	20 years
$800	$48,000	$96,000	$144,000	$192,000
$900	$54,000	$108,000	$162,000	$216,000
$1,000	$60,000	$120,000	$180,000	$240,000
$2,000	$120,000	$240,000	$360,000	$480,000

Who gets My money?

LANDLORD
GROCER
MILKMAN
DOCTOR
DENTIST
TAX COLLECTOR
CREDITOR
CLOTHER
ME, IF THERE IS ANY LEFT

The sooner you start to save, the more money you will have for your retirement. You will also have the peace of mind knowing that if you have a fiscal emergency, there is always this back-up. You will be able to borrow money at a lesser rate for financing a car or home.

A Case Study

I have neighbors, both thirty years old, each of whom smokes a carton (ten packs) of cigarettes a week. They also drink a case of beer a week. What is wrong with this picture?

The cigarettes cost approximately $60 for the two cartons. The beer averages out at $20 a week. The grand total comes to $80/week x 52 weeks = $4,160.00 per year. Multiply this by twenty, thirty, or forty years. (See the Rule of 72 in the next chapter.)

Now suppose that smoking and drinking the beer did not impair their health. Let us further suppose that they keep up this pace for forty years until they are seventy. Further suppose that both are now retired and have no income, except for Social Security. Keep in mind, though, that Social Security is not intended to take care of all a person's needs and will not do so in thirty years either.

So let's assume they didn't smoke or didn't drink beer but diligently saved the $80 each and every week for the forty years and invested that money all these years with a guaranteed return of 6 percent. Look what the financial returns would have brought them and what a wonderful retirement they would have had.

The moral of this case study is: Start now and save whatever you can rather than blow smoke. Remember, there is no guarantee that your government will assist you in your old age.

Think of what you can do with the secure feeling that as time goes on you will have a larger and larger nest egg, which over the years can be compounding the dollars you have already saved. Should you have a financial emergency, you can borrow the money you need because it is money you have saved. There may come a time when you wish to go into business with this nest egg. If you have a son or daughter who plans to go to college, this could be the difference between being able to help or not.

Recent Grads Need Financial Guidance

Michelle Singletary, *The Washington Post*, 8 May 2005

Soon college graduates will be heading into their first full-time jobs. I wonder how many will be able to adequately address the laundry list of decisions they'll have to make about their personal finances. I asked a group of seniors recently a battery of questions just to test how many might be prepared. "Who can tell me what a 401(k) plan is?" Blank stares. After some prompting, many said they had heard of a 401(k) plan but couldn't really say how it worked.

"What about an IRA, do you know what that stands for and what it is?" In a class of about 25, only one young lady knew. The rest—blank stares. None of the students knew that these were long term tax deferred savings plans. I continued: "Do you have a plan to pay down your student debt? What about housing, do you know about how much you should spend on rent? At your age and stage of life, which is more important: life insurance or disability insurance? How much should you have saved up in case of an emergency? Where should you park your emergency money? Do you have a credit card and, if so, why it is important not to max out the card?"

Still nothing but blank stares.

I know some of the questions are tough. But it's downright tragic that so many young folks have spent so much time and money getting an education, and yet that training mostly has failed to include required courses in basic money management.

Our institutions of higher learning prepare them to get jobs but, unfortunately, many graduates won't know how to handle the money they will earn on those jobs.

I hope as parents, grandparents, uncles and aunts, you'll realize your job isn't done yet. While you're preparing to celebrate the big achievement of a young adult in your family, take the graduate aside after the party and give him or her the information or resources (if you don't know yourself) to make smart money decisions.

Not sure where to start? Here's a list of the top personal finance advice I would give:

Don't rush to rent. I don't think every person graduating from college needs to get a place of his or her own. It's not a sign of failure if they need to come home for some financial peace and relief. Young people are graduating with an incredible amount of student debt load. Give them a break. Perhaps the best thing financially for them is to live at home for a year or two (or three or four) while they save up so that, once they do move out, they won't have to come back.

Automate your savings. Before I left for work on the first day of my first full-time job at a newspaper in Baltimore, my grandmother, Big Mama, sat me down at the kitchen table and gave me advice that set the stage for me to become a lifetime saver.

"Shell, when you get to work, march your behind up to the payroll department and sign up for a credit union account," Big Mama said sternly. "Make sure before you get your hands on a single penny of your paycheck that you put some money away in that account. And don't touch it unless you absolutely have to. Do this one thing and for the rest of your life you will always have a piece of money."

I've followed that advice for my entire adult life, and I've always had a stash of cash. So advise your graduate, as a start, to put away enough savings to eventually cover three months of living expenses. The expenses should cover what it costs them to live every month (student loan repayment, credit card payments, car insurance, etc.). And because this is emergency money it should be kept in a savings account or some other deposit account to protect the principal.

Tell them to start investing for retirement now. Stay on them to fill out the paperwork for their company's retirement plan. And when I say stay on them, I mean nag, badger, plead or beg them until they do it.

Remind them that the one thing they have on their side is time and the sooner they begin investing the more they will have at retirement. Be sure to tell them to invest at least enough to get all the matching money their employer is willing to add to the pot (i.e., free money). Tell them the importance of diversification. Diversification of investment is probably the most important thing a young investor can do. Tell them not to be too conservative in their investment choices. After all, they do have five or six decades to let their money work for them.

If their employer does not offer a retirement plan, help them set up an IRA account. If you're not sure how to explain what an IRA is, go to www.investopedia.com. You will find a wealth of basic investing information.

Encourage them to get disability insurance. Many young adults make the mistake of thinking life insurance is more important than disability insurance. The fact is they are more likely to become disabled and need that insurance rather than life insurance.

Remember that life insurance is supposed to take care of your dependents should you die. If no one is depending on a worker's income to survive, then that worker doesn't need life insurance right now.

If the employer offers disability insurance coverage, new workers should get enough to replace at least 60 percent to 70 percent of their income while they are off the job.

These are just a few things college graduates or any other newcomers to the work force need to consider (and we all know there are more). Help a graduate get the right financial start in this new stage of their life by helping them become smart about their money.

If you live in a northern climate and want the winter to go by quickly, go to the bank in November and take out a promissory note which will come due the following spring.

Now turn to the next chapter on investing for the future.

Chapter 4

Investing for Your Future

TIME IS RUNNING

START NOW

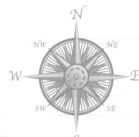

WHEN IS THE best time to start a savings plan? Most everyone will say ASAP. You agree, but your first question is or should be, where shall I invest?

An insurance salesman will say, "Invest with me, and I will protect your family, and, if you become short of cash, you can borrow some or all of the cash value that builds each year." This is true, but if by chance you needed to borrow on this policy, which is usually an ordinary life policy, your family would receive, in the case of your premature death, the full amount as stated on your life insurance policy, less what you borrowed.

Let us take this a little further. When you bought the policy, it was:

- For protection
- For savings
- For retirement

Yes, you could borrow the money, but, if you did, you would have to pay interest during the time you had possession of the money. Taking this analysis a step further, let us assume you are now sixty-five and wish to retire. You advise the insurance company of your intention, and now the big surprise: You must still pay the premiums for thirty-five years. If you stopped paying them, you would have no more insurance. You could have whatever cash value remains, and that would be your retirement.

So, you did not have the three items the policy said you had but only one. Add to this the fact that you have paid a lot of premiums to become a partner with the insurance company.

Now let us talk to the mutual fund salesman. He seems to be a nice young fellow, full of life and all kinds of ideas about the stock market. He tells you about how individuals became rich in short order by buying on an up market and selling out at the right time. This may have been the truth. Did he also tell you about those who invested and lost all? No, he probably gave you statistics about the average return on your money over a period of years. Also true.

Now it is decision time. Do I buy an ordinary life insurance policy or take a shot at the market and with any luck retire early?

A third man comes into the picture and says, "I can show you the best of both worlds." This makes you perk up, and you listen with great intensity as the man says, "We will give you all the life insurance necessary for your family to be comfortable in the case of your sudden demise. The insurance will cost very little because it is what we call term insurance or pure insurance." You never get any monies back, you cannot borrow against the policy, and it has no cash value. If you take the money that either gentleman suggested, however, pay a premium for the pure insurance, and invest the balance in a group of stocks on a monthly basis (which is called dollar cost averaging), the odds are that you will be able to retire at the age you pick.

I recommend the third option.

The previous chapter focused on cutting expenses and saving for your future. Now you must invest these savings somewhere. Where is "somewhere"? I am not a stockbroker, nor am I a financial advisor, but I wish to give you some food for thought based on some of my own experiences.

How much you want or are able to save and how often you will be able to add to these savings are the questions at hand. Placing one sum of money in an investment and then forgetting about it is probably not a really good investment. Conversely, if you put a certain amount away each month or as often as you can, i.e., weekly, biweekly, or monthly, as long as you get into the habit of staying with it, you will see constant growth of your money. Your ending balance might fluctuate, but the arrow will generally point upward.

When starting out on your investing, don't take on unknown stocks, especially those without a proven history. Don't put all your eggs in one basket. Find and choose a good financial advisor just as you would choose a doctor or lawyer. Your advisor can and will keep you up-to-date on any market changes. Stick to what you know and leave the investment to someone who is in the business full-time. You don't do your own plumbing or electrical work, so why do your own investing? Advisors generally recommend individual stocks, but investing directly in low-cost index funds with Vanguard or Fidelity is so much more diversified and much less expensive. Mutual Fund Money Market Funds always beat bank deposits.

Try to stay in for the long haul. Your investment portfolio won't make you rich in one year, but over a period of time you should see continued financial growth.

Beware of scams and get-rich-quick schemes. If it sounds too good to be true, it probably is.

Keep in mind that at or about the age of sixty-five, you should be entitled to draw some of the monies that you and your employer have paid into the Social Security Trust Fund. It was never intended to be enough for you to retire on without any other savings.

The brutal, cold fact is that it is probably one of the biggest—if not the biggest—scam ever perpetrated on the American people.

Just ask your congressman or senator what happens to the monies you and your employer have paid into this Social Security Trust Fund, which doesn't have any money in it because Congress borrowed these monies, supposedly in trust, and gave an "I owe you" as collateral.

Another part of the scam is that both congressmen and senators have a pension plan that boggles the mind as to how much they draw for retirement after serving just one term. In some cases they can expect in excess of a million dollars or more.

The Essence of Having a Checking Account

Whether you are a business person or an individual, if you don't have a checking account, you should.

It is good business to deposit all your income in the bank or a savings and loan company. The reasons for this are many:

1. Keeping loose cash around makes it tempting for people to steal. It is much easier to keep track of all business transactions by check rather than cash.

2. You have peace of mind knowing you have ready access to cash, checks, and money orders.

3. As long as you maintain a small working balance, there will be little charge for this service.

4. Use the bank account properly (i.e., depositing all monies and disbursing the same).

5. At the year end, you will have almost everything you need for filing your income taxes.

6. In your checkbook you will have a running journal that lists all your deposits (monies in) and your disbursements (monies out) in easy-to-read, sequential order. Try to keep these records clean and up-to-date.

On the following sheet are pictures of a check with instructions on how to fill it out. There is also a bank reconciliation form, which will show you all the checks you have written, cashed or un-cashed.

Elements

1. **Account name and address**
2. **Payee (to whom check is being paid)**
3. **Bank name**
4. **Bank number**
5. **Written amount**
6. **Account number**
7. **Payer's signature**
8. **Current date**
9. **Consecutive number**
10. **Bank transit routing symbol**

# of a Check

You can easily balance your CHECKBOOK by doing these things.

Fill in below the amounts shown in your BANK STATEMENT and on your CHECKBOOK.

| Balance shown on BANK STATEMENT | $ _____ | Balance shown on CHECKBOOK | $ _____ |

| Add deposits not on BANK STATEMENT | $ _____ | Add any deposits not already entered in CHECKBOOK | $ _____ |

| | Total $ _____ | | Total $ _____ |

| Subtract checks issued, but not on BANK STATEMENT. $ _____ | | Subtract service charges and other bank charges not in CHECKBOOK $ _____ | |

| | Total $ _____ | | Total $ _____ |
| | BALANCE $ _____ | | BALANCE $ _____ |

The balance of your bank statement should equal the balance of your checkbook

Combining Mutual Funds and Life Insurance for Financial Security

Few persons achieve financial security, although all persons want it. The Social Security Board states that at age sixty-five, people

- depend on relatives: 45% of the time
- depend on charity: 30% of the time
- are still working: 23% of the time.
- Only 2% are self-sustaining.

Why life insurance and mutual funds?

Ordinary life insurance is a combination of death benefits and savings.

In an ordinary life policy, unless it is voluntarily terminated by the insured, premium payments are made until death or age ninety-six, whichever comes first, at which time the policy matures. As indicated, ordinary life insurance contains a savings feature so that money is gradually accumulated in cash values. At age thirty-five, a typical life insurance policy might have a premium of $17.85 per $1,000. In its tenth year, the cash value of the policy would be $135.17; in its fifteenth year, $227.58; in its twentieth $323.02; and in its thirtieth, $512.49.

Mutual funds generally are the safest way to get into equities.

Full-time professional management of a selected list of securities answers the bothersome problem of when to sell as well as when to buy, and, if desired, there is automatic reinvestment of dividends and capital gains.

Dollar cost averaging can be employed and by doing so on a fluctuating market (and all markets fluctuate), you automatically buy more shares when the market is down and fewer when the market is up (the reverse of most investors).

Safety: Mutual funds operate in a governmental "fish bowl" of regulations aimed at investor safety.

Liquidity: Your fund shares can be redeemed at net asset value at any time.

Rule of 72

I'd like to show you a mathematical quirk called the "Rule of 72." In order to find out how long it would take to double money, you have to know one of two things. If you wish to know how long it takes to double money by compounding it at a rate of return, divide the rate of return into 72, and the answer will tell us how many years it will take. For example: a 6 percent return divided into 72 means it will take twelve years to double if it is compounded. And in reverse, if we wish to double money in a number of years, we divide the years into 72, and the answer gives us the rate of return at which we must compound. For example: Twelve years divided into 72 gives us 6 percent.

In order to see what the actual differences are in rates of returns, let us apply some rates of return and some years to a sum of money. I will give you $10,000. Now, let's see what the results would be:

Rule of 72

Rate of Return	2%	4%	6%	12%
6 years				$ 20,000
12 years			$20,000	$ 40,000
18 years		$20,000		$ 80,000
24 years			$40,000	$160,000
30 years				$320,000
36 years	$20,000	$40,000	$80,000	$640,000

The rule basically says that if you know the number of years, you can determine the rate of return or vice versa.

At 2 percent, by applying the rule of 72, we see it would take thirty-six years for $10,000 to double. At 4 percent, it would double in eighteen years and double again in thirty-six years for a total of $40,000. At 6 percent, it would double once in twelve years, double again in twenty-four, and a third time in thirty-six for a total of $80,000. Though 6 percent appears to be 50 percent more than 4 percent, we see that by adding years and compounding, your $10,000 would net $70,000 at 6 percent as opposed to just $30,000 at 4 percent—more than a 100 percent difference. At 12 percent, your $10,000 would double every six years to reach a total of $640,000 in thirty-six years. All of the first three rates, 2, 4, and 6 percent could be obtained today as a guaranteed return, couldn't they? If you had $10,000 and received a guaranteed rate of 6 percent, do you believe your $80,000 would be enough to retire on thirty-six years from today? Probably not. In this case, the guarantee is also a guarantee that we shall fail to reach our retirement needs. Unfortunately, I can't tell you where you can get a guaranteed return of 12 percent, but I'd like to tell you a story now that I hope will give you some ideas about where you might be able to accumulate money at a higher rate than the guaranteed returns we have today.

This is about the affluent society we live in today. There are two keys to affluence. Those keys are "faith" and "specialists." Let's talk about faith first and the fact that we must have faith today or our lives would have little meaning. We must have faith in the future, in this great country of ours, in our jobs, our families, and in ourselves. We even have to have faith in the fact we will wake up tomorrow, don't we? You see, our whole life is based on faith. And we do live in an age of specialists. For example: If your car breaks down, you don't call the plumber, do you? And if you have a toothache, you don't call the auto mechanic. When we have problems, we call the specialist, don't we? So we live in an age of specialists, and I'll talk more about that fact later on. We try to predict our future by what has happened in the past. One of the gauges we use is the gross national product (GNP). The GNP is the value of all the goods and services produced in the United States in a given year.

Our economy continues to grow as does our population, which has reached the 300 million mark.

Today there seems to be more of everything: more people, more roads, more cars, more buildings, more children's toys, and more children as our population grows older.

There is, however, a flip side to this picture. Rising product costs create inflation, which is defined as an increase in the volume of money and credit relative to available goods, resulting in a substantial and continuing rise in the general price level.

So, let us turn again to your future. The sooner you know the direction you are going, in terms of your job, family, residence, and savings, the more independent and satisfied your life should become. Not all persons find happiness in life, but you can if you try. Forget yesterday; it is gone forever; live for today, and plan for tomorrow.

Remember, money isn't everything, but it beats whatever comes in second. That said, how you earn it and dispose of it are two factors that should guide you through life.

The world is changing so quickly that it is mentally and physically hard to keep up. It is predicted that people currently twenty years of age will change jobs and/or careers three or more times during their lives. What about you? Will you be prepared? I stress again and again that one must read and keep learning, or this world will pass you by.

The American Dream

How to become a millionaire or, at least, how to live like one. At this time, I would like to introduce you to Charlie Brown. Charlie Brown is the kind of guy who never did anything right in his life. Every decision he ever made was wrong. He was the born loser. A foof! Well, one day when Charlie was forty years old, he was out at the racetrack and won $10,000. Remember, I said Charlie never did anything right in his life, and that day he wasn't at the racetrack with his banker or his life insurance man. He was with a lousy mutual fund salesman. And before Charlie got away, that lousy mutual fund salesman talked Charlie out of his $10,000.

When Charlie got home and told Mrs. Brown what had happened, she blew her stack. She said, "Charlie, you never did anything right in your life. Everything you do is wrong. You are a, a, a foof." Well, Charlie felt pretty bad. There was little he could do about it, and besides, that lousy mutual fund salesman had charged him $800. So he kind of forgot about it. If Charlie had forgotten about his $10,000 for twenty-five years, his $10,000 plus twenty-five years times professional management would have accumulated to $226,802. Then he would have been known as "C. Brown, Investor." But remember, Charlie never did anything right in his life. And he didn't do this either.

Along about the time he was fifty-five, he decided he wanted to join the country club, travel a little, and do some fishing, so he needed more monthly income. He remembered his $10,000 and called that mutual fund salesman to see whether he still had anything left. The mutual fund salesman checked and found Charlie's $10,000 plus fifteen years times professional management had grown to $83,285, and it had only cost him $800. Charlie was really surprised. But all he wanted at that time was to go to his mailbox once a month to get a check. The mutual fund salesman said he could arrange that. So Charlie started receiving a check in the amount of $416.43 per month, or almost $5,000 per year, and during the next ten years Charlie got almost $50,000. Now Charlie was sixty-five, and what do you suppose he did?

What do most people do when they reach age sixty-five? Retire? Not Charlie. He died! And when Mrs. Brown checked with the mutual fund salesman to see whether Charlie had any money left after using up almost $50,000 of his $83,000, that wonderful mutual fund salesman checked and found Charlie still had $142,390 left.

The moral of this story is that if Charlie hadn't been at the racetrack with that mutual fund salesman that day, he would probably have spent his $10,000. And chances are good that in a few years not many people would have remembered Charlie Brown. But Mrs. Brown will remember Charlie, and she has seen to it that people won't forget him. She has erected a sort of monument in fond memory of "Charles R. Brown, Esquire." In order to have a better understanding of what Charlie Brown did, we must have an idea of how our capitalistic system works.

I'd like to ask you some questions. Where is the safest place we could put our money and still earn a return? US Bonds. Where does the government get the money to pay the interest on these bonds? Taxes. Who buys bonds? People. How do most people get the money to buy bonds? By working for corporations. Who pays taxes? People and corporations. In essence, that means that in reality the US Bonds are only as safe as the hundred thousand-plus corporations that help support the government.

Investing should be a part of your life's plan. The next part is insuring your family, so if the bread winner is unable to work or, worse, meets an untimely death, the family will be protected.

("The American Dream" was presented in a finance course I took in the 1950s.)

Chapter 5

Insurance

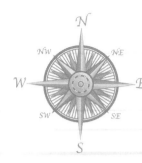

Why Does This Person Buy Insurance?

BECAUSE ON A morning during the days of his youth, he overheard just enough of a discussion between his mother and father together that they had borrowed money to pay his tuition to the university, and he determined forthwith that they would be repaid.

Because one soft summer evening, the most wonderful girl in the world shyly promised herself to him and him alone so long as they both should live, and he vowed to himself that, no matter what might come, she would never regret placing her future in his hands.

Because one bright morning, a building contractor handed him two shiny keys on a wire and pronounced the exciting words, "She's finished and all yours," and he swore that no quirk of fate would ever drive his bride from this, their home.

Because in the predawn hush of a wintry day, the first thin wail of a newborn babe calmed his nervous pacing with the solemn realization that he and that wonderful woman had created a new life, and he pledged to himself right then and there that no child of theirs would lack all the training and preparation the world of tomorrow might demand.

Because one never-to-be-forgotten midnight, his next-door neighbor died, and he spent the endless hours until morning trying to comfort and reassure the widow, who was wholly incapable of comprehending or coping with the economic facts of life. He resolved that should he be the first to die in his household, his widow would be as free from money worries and the necessity of money management as was humanly possible to arrange.

Because on his fortieth birthday, when he and two other men pooled their resources and established their own business, he insisted that prudent arrangements be made for the protection of the three families involved and of the business in the event of one partner's death.

Because as he grew older, he realized more and more that the day would come when he would have to step aside for a younger man, and he promised himself that when that fateful day arrived, he would be prepared to retire with dignity.

It is for reasons such as these that life insurance is purchased—simple, elementary reasons, which spring with impelling force from the hearts of responsible men. Whatever your reason may be, there is no time like the present to protect your family and all your assets, large or small.

As a footnote to the above, I had the privilege to comfort two ladies (both in their seventies) who suddenly became widows. Upon reviewing their assets and data for filing their taxes, I found neither had any savings and neither any life insurance. Need I say more?

Last Will and Testament

"To the Great Northern Insurance Company
I Bequeath the Cash Value of All My Life Insurance Policies."

Life insurance is a wonderful thing. There is no substitute for it. But it is probably the most misused thing in America.

That misuse is born of a wide misunderstanding of the real purpose of life insurance—to provide protection. Now, before you say, "Oh, everyone knows that's the purpose of life insurance," let me assure you that everyone doesn't know it—or knowing it, they don't remember when they are ready to buy.

Many of you buy life insurance to pay off the mortgage or to educate or to retire at age sixty-five. Give a modern life insurance salesperson half a chance, and you will have life insurance doing everything but sweeping out your kitchen.

Life insurance was never intended to do these things. It was intended to provide you with an estate if you don't live long enough to accumulate one yourself.

When you insure your home or your car, you give the insurance company just the cost of protection. You wouldn't think of handing the company an extra hundred dollars to hold off with the understanding that it was to be given back to you at some future date. If you want a savings account, you open one with a savings bank, not with an insurance company.

When you buy life insurance, you are insuring your future income against your dying before you have time to earn it. This is the same "protection" job done by the insurance you bought on your house or your car—and you should give the company just the cost of insuring you, not another penny. Remember, it's an insurance company and not a bank.

It is essential for every individual to understand this important fact and guide himself accordingly because life insurance companies encourage you to regard them as both a savings bank and an insurance company.

There are two types of life insurance—term insurance (which is pure protection) and all other kinds. The "other kinds" all consist of some combination of term insurance plus a savings account maturing at some date in the future.

Whole life, ordinary life, straight life—all different names for the same thing—consist of term insurance plus a savings account that matures when you are ninety-six. "Twenty payment life" or "thirty payment life" are similar except that instead of paying until you die (or until the policy matures), you crowd the lifetime of premiums into the first twenty or thirty years. That way, if you die at seventy-five, the company doesn't have to lose all the premiums you would have paid if you had lived to age ninety-six—you obligingly prepaid them. Obviously, the chances of your living until the maturity of the policy are pretty slim——actually, about one in 850,000.

Policies that provide for the savings account to mature early enough to offer the purchaser some reasonable hope of living long enough to get his or her savings account back are called "endowment policies." Policies sold to educate children are fifteen- or seventeen-year endowments—term insurance plus a savings account that matures when your youngster is ready for college. Retirement income policies consist of term insurance plus a savings account that matures when you're between sixty and sixty-five and is automatically applied to the purchase of an annuity.

No one will quarrel with the idea of providing protection for one's family while at the same time accumulating a fund for some such purpose as education or retirement.

The incredible thing about this "package" of protection plus a savings account offered by the insurance companies is that if you die, the company keeps your savings account.

Let's illustrate: You have a $100,000, twenty-year endowment—actually a twenty-year term insurance policy plus a savings account that matures for $100,000 at the end of that time. The savings account is called "the cash value." Each year, you give the company the cost of the protection—and some extra dollars to be put away for you until the end of the twenty years. You've had the policy for fifteen years. Your savings account with the company has accumulated to $67,500. That's your money, the accumulation of extra dollars you need never to have given the company in the first place.

You die. The company pays the beneficiary the $100,000 face amount of the policy (the "protection" for which you gave them a premium this year)—and they keep your $67,500 savings account! The only way you can get that savings account back is by living right up to the very last day of the twenty years. If you die in the nineteenth year, when the savings account has grown to $95,000, the company will pay the $100,000 of insurance—and keep your $95,000 savings account.

Consider that ordinary life policy you own. Each year until you are age ninety-six, you will give the company the cost of the protection plus some extra dollars to be salted away in the savings account. To collect that savings account, you must stick around—and keep paying premiums—until your ninety-sixth birthday. If you die before then, even one day before, the company will pay the insurance for which you gave them a premium that year—and they'll pocket your savings account. Seriously now, would you go down to a bank and open a savings account with the understanding that if you died before age ninety-six that the bank could keep your money? You wouldn't? Why, then, would you do it with the insurance company?

Whenever you need to use some of the money you've accumulated in your savings account with the insurance company, you may borrow it back at two or three times the interest rate at which you are lending it to them. If a savings bank offered you 2 ½ percent interest and suggested that if you needed the money at any time, it would lend it back to you at 6 percent interest, you'd leave immediately, taking your money with you. "Fancy them offering to lend me back my own money for three times what I'm lending it to them for!" you'd exclaim. If you wouldn't think of doing it with a savings bank, why would you do it with an insurance company?

If you become aware of the inequity of this loan arrangement and inform the insurance company you won't borrow back your own money, you'll just take the savings account out altogether, the company will say, "If you do, we'll cancel your protection." You must take either the loan value or the cash value; if you take the latter, the company will cancel your policy.

You'd be much better off if you just bought term insurance in the first place and put the difference in premium in the savings bank. By any given date in the future, you'd accumulate more in your savings account, because insurance companies pay out 15 percent of everything you pay in your lifetime just for selling the policy, including 15 percent of the savings account. If you buy term insurance and put the difference in the savings bank, the latter won't pay anyone for selling you a savings account. All this money will be added to your savings account. And if you die, your family will have all the term insurance plus all the money in the savings bank. You'll be better off if you live, and your family will be better off if you die.

Dig out your insurance policies tonight and look up the table headed "cash value." That's it; that's your savings account. That's what the insurance company will inherit if you die tomorrow.

You don't have to be very smart to figure out that if you cancel that $100,000 policy and put the $70,000 cash value into the savings bank, and go out and buy $100,000 of term insurance, your family will have the same $100,000 total if you die—and you'll be paying the premium of only $3,000 of insurance instead of $10,000.

Of course, if you're a financial jellyfish who can't save money unless the insurance company takes it away from you, you'd better stick with the insurance. But you should at least realize the high price you're paying for your weakness.

If you do have the intestinal fortitude to save your own money, take a good, long look at your life insurance tonight. Figure out what your "savings account" has grown to—and decide whether you want the insurance company or your family to get it when you die.

Right now, you're running the risk of losing that savings account completely if you die or of having inflation melt away its real value if you do live long enough to get it back.

Consider instead whether you should not accept the risks—and the rewards—of putting your money to work in a program of careful, systematic investment completely separate and apart from your life insurance protection. Then tomorrow, make two phone calls. With the first, make a date to talk about some low-rate term insurance. Then call someone who sells mutual funds and ask him or her to suggest a suitable investment for that $7,000 cash value and for the money you'll save on life insurance premiums every year from now on.

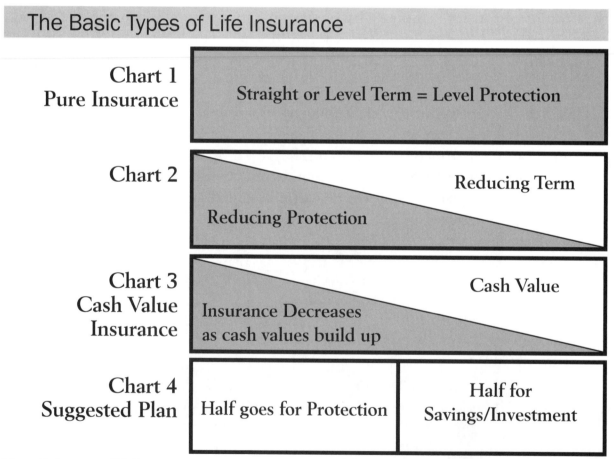

The Basic Types of Life Insurance

**Chart 1
Pure Insurance** — Straight or Level Term = Level Protection

Chart 2 — Reducing Protection / Reducing Term

**Chart 3
Cash Value
Insurance** — Insurance Decreases as cash values build up / Cash Value

**Chart 4
Suggested Plan** — Half goes for Protection / Half for Savings/Investment

Note: I do not sell life insurance or securities. Buying life insurance will be your decision. Learn about it before you invest.

Basic Life Insurance Principles

Although insurance companies offer a number of policy variations, in the final analysis there is only one kind of life insurance—*term insurance.*

Every policy is either term by itself or term plus a long-range savings plan. Term insurance by itself will either be *level term* as per Chart 1 or *reducing term* as per Chart 2.

Both of these are forms of pure protection that can run for a period of one to twenty years or until you reach the age of sixty-five or seventy.

Naturally, the longer the period is to run, the higher the premium per year per $1,000 of coverage. The reason is that the company is to provide protection in the face amount for the whole period at the same initial rate. The premium for a five- or ten-year term is much less than that for a twenty-year term, but whenever your client renews it, the premium will jump.

Chart 1—we have an example of straight or *level term.*

The premium is fixed for the period the policy is to run, and the amount of actual protection provided is also constant.

Chart 2—we have an example of *reducing term,* or sometimes called "decreasing term" by companies. This coverage, like the level term, can be bought for varying periods of time during which the amount of protection diminishes while the premium remains constant. This premium is much cheaper than that for level term insurance because as you grow older and the mortality hazard increases, the insurance diminishes, and the company therefore gradually reduces its risk.

The *reducing term* is the foundation of every type of cash value policy, regardless of the name the insurance company gives it. Whether it be *ordinary life,* a twenty-year *payment life, endowment,* or whatever, decreasing term insurance is a part of it.

Chart 3—this facet of reducing term coupled with a cash value type of policy is illustrated. The reducing term decreases gradually until at maturity it has been completely replaced by the savings account element in the policy.

Chart 4—we have illustrated what we consider a suggested alternate plan, which separates the protection from the savings element. This is done by using what the person insured would normally spend for a cash value type of policy and dividing said amount between the reducing term and the type of investment.

Term insurance is the foundation of every life insurance policy. Hence, you can dismiss as immaterial all of an agent's arguments against term. Except for certain pensions or deferred compensation plans and cross purchase agreements, term insurance can suffice.

The next time you purchase a life insurance policy, have the salesman answer the following questions before you buy:

1. Does my beneficiary receive the face amount of the insurance plus the cash value if I should die?

2. If my beneficiary does not receive the cash value, in addition to the face amount of the insurance, when I die, who will receive it?

3. If the cash value equals my savings, why must I pay interest to borrow my own money?

4. If I borrow my cash value, will my beneficiary still receive the full face amount of the insurance if I should die? If not, why?

5. If my cash values are earning 2 ½% to 3 ½% per year, can you guarantee that this money will have the same purchasing power as it did when I put it into this contract?

6. If I am earning dividends, why are they non-taxable? Also, why are the premiums per thousand dollars of protection often higher on contracts that pay dividends than on ones that do not?

7. What is my cost per thousand dollars of protection on my existing contract at my present age?

The Three-Legged Stool

This three-legged stool is not for you to sit on.

It was designed to put you into a comfortable and satisfying retirement:

Leg #1 is Social Security. No one can predict the future, so don't think you can know how much money your government will give you in your retirement years.

Leg #2 is an employer-sponsored retirement plan. Any plan you now participate in may or may not last over your working lifetime. Businesses are sold or may go out of business. So we turn to the third leg:

Leg #3 is personal savings and investments. If you do not start a savings plan immediately, you will have no one to blame except yourself if you cannot retire comfortably. Regardless of the amount you put away for your retirement years, just do something today.

The following are places you should consider placing your investment monies: banks, savings and loans, mutual funds, and real estate.

On Insurance Policies

Review your insurance policies at least every three years. This may save you money, get you more coverage, or both.

As you become more knowledgeable about all kinds of insurance, you are almost certain to save more monies than anticipated.

If now you understand the necessity of saving, and invest these savings, plus make sure you have ample life insurance, you have almost guaranteed yourself and your family a pleasant retirement, without financial worry.

Now that we have covered what you will face when you graduate, sit back, read, and enjoy the good life.

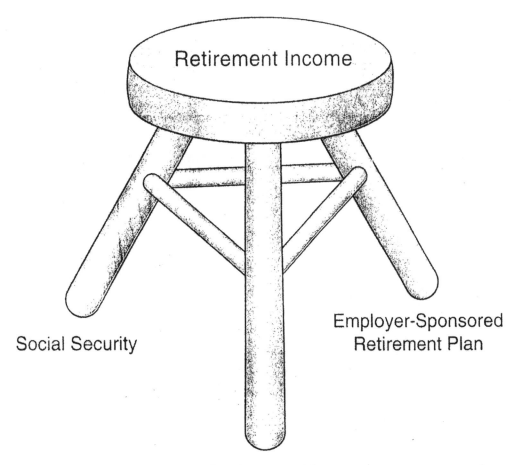

Chapter 6

Health

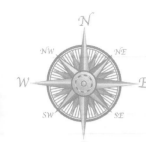

Everything in Moderation (E.I.M.)

"AN APPLE A day keeps the doctor away."

When I talk about Everything in Moderation (E.I.M.), this should or could be the goal of every person, starting today. New Year's resolutions are one thing, but many fall by the wayside during the first few months, and by six months few people, if any, have stuck to their goals.

Okay, you say to yourself, "I tried, but too many things got in my way."

This is a very, very important subject, so let's start with one word: "health." Now let's make it two words: "your health."

You ask, "What does this have to do with the day after graduation?" The answer is: "Everything." In most cases when you leave school, you leave home. So? Who is going to remind you to visit your dentist twice a year? You should do this yourself. If you do this very simple thing, it will be a big factor in keeping good health. A word to the wise should be sufficient.

Taking care of your teeth is one thing; how about the rest of your body? You say you feel fine now, but what do you do when you don't feel fine? E.I.M. suggests you visit your medical doctor at least once for an annual checkup. Yes, it does cost money, but having your body parts checked, e.g., eyes, ears, nose, throat, heart, and whatever else you may need, could save your life. A word to the wise should be sufficient.

Now I wish to talk to you about another of the most important things in your life: *food*. Without it you die. With too much or the wrong kinds of food, the quality of your life could be diminished and its length shortened. Statistics show that violation of basic good nutrition recommendations can cause you to pay a severe penalty. Diabetes, kidney failure, or a host of other ailments could cost you pain and money.

Fast foods are becoming a curse on the American people and spreading rapidly throughout the rest of the world. Sure, it is quick and easy to drop in for a burger, fries, and a shake or a soda, but check the calories in that food. Step on the scale and watch the weight move upward.

At least two things happen to you:

1. You will gain weight, maybe not today, *but you will gain weight*. Men usually get a pot belly, and women can get wide hips. If you gain too much, you will need expensive new clothes, not always very stylish. And other dangers are waiting in the wings: high blood pressure and/or diabetes.

2. The next part of the story is about finances. If you pack a light lunch instead of dropping into your favorite fast food place, you could save a good amount of money. Average cost for lunch at the burger place could be about ten dollars, give or take a few. That for a five-day work or school week would amount to $50 every week. Project that out to fifty-two weeks a year, and it becomes $2,400. Think of it—if you had put the same amount in a savings account at the bank, you would have over $2,500 to use as you see fit.

Do this for a few years along with your other savings, and you will surprise yourself at how fast your money grows.

Thousands of books about health are available along with educational CDs. You won't have much need for them if you follow our simple rule about E.I.M.

If your attitude is mostly positive and pleasant, statistics show you will live longer. So why not do it right? Exercise every day for at least thirty minutes a day and you will live longer and enjoy the good life.

As a man once said, "If I had known I would live so long, I would have taken better care of myself." Funny, yes, but true!

If you really want the good life, there is a price to pay. And the cost is not the same for all persons. For instance, if you save a certain amount of money each week, you should have security in your old age.

Here is another three-legged stool: first leg: how you dress; second leg: your attitude; third leg: how well you communicate.

DRESS   ATTITUDE   COMMUNICATION

Which leg would you say is the most important?

The answer is—they are equally important. Why?

Without all three working together, the stool cannot stand on its own.

Think about it:

You may dress well and have a good attitude but cannot communicate.

You may have a good attitude and good communication skills, but you may dress like a slob.

You may dress and communicate well, but your attitude is for the birds.

Keep in mind that you need all three to become successful.

Chapter 7

Decisions, Decisions

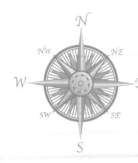

QUESTION: HAVE YOU ever been taught how to make decisions? If your answer is no, you are not alone.

"Decision" is a noun. The following definitions are taken from *Webster's Concise College Dictionary*:

1. The act or process of deciding.

2. The act of making up one's mind: a difficult decision.

3. Something that is decided, resolution.

4. A judgment as one pronounced by a court.

5. The quality of being decided, firmness; to speak with decision.

6. The final score in any sport or contest.

7. The awarding of a victory in a boxing match when there is no knockout based on scoring by the referee and judges.

So let us start at the top. Every day of your life is about making decisions.

Your first decision after you awaken is whether or not to get out of bed.

Your second decision is what clothes to wear.

Perhaps your next decision will be to do exercises or eat breakfast.

Suppose you have chores to do. Do you decide to do them now, after school, or after you get home from your job?

For example, let's say your chore is to fix dinner. What will you serve, how much will you cook, and what time will your meal be served for the rest of the family? And so it goes. Decisions, decisions, decisions, into the night until you finally decide to go to bed. At that time you undress, turn off the TV, and go to bed.

A short but basically true story I heard many years ago was this: A vagrant was walking down a country road, and it was getting near lunch time. He stopped and asked a farmer whether he could get some food from him. The farmer said, "Yes, but I have to go into town to buy some merchandise, and on my return we will eat. In the meantime, while I am gone, would you be so kind as to sort this pile of potatoes into three piles, small, medium, and large?" "Sure," said the man and started to work. An hour later the farmer returned, and each pile had only four or five potatoes in it. The farmer said, "What were you doing while I was gone?" The man said, "Decisions, decisions."

Maturity to Make Decisions

After you have made a decision, regardless of the consequences, don't fret over it if it was the wrong one. We all make mistakes, some small ones, some big. It's too late to cry over spilled milk—just try to learn from it and not do it again. The temptation may be there, but discretion should be the better part of valor. Yes, we can all do better if we try. It does take fortitude to keep on the straight and narrow path, but the end results usually are worth it.

The biggest waste of all is not making any decision while the world passes you by. How many times have you heard a person say, "If I had only bought that stock when it was low," or "Why didn't I invest with my neighbor, who invented this new gadget? Some additional financial help was needed, and now he is a millionaire, and I am still poor." Remember, investments of all kinds are available at all times. Don't invest unless you can afford it, because you could lose part or all of it. There are no guarantees in life except death and taxes.

The above all depends on whether you decide to save and invest your money. It's all about *decisions*.

Maturity to make decisions is based on experience; experience comes from making mistakes, and that is what makes experience.

I Offer This Experience to You Now

Consider World War II, when the invasion of Europe was imminent. General Dwight Eisenhower was the Supreme Allied Commander of all the invasion forces. Every day he had to make hundreds of decisions but never one so great as what day to pick for the invasion. He knew that thousands of young American and Allied soldiers would be killed or wounded during the invasion. He also knew that thousands more would die during continued fighting. But the decision had to be made. The rest is history.

Perhaps you have struggled for some time with trying to make a major decision but cannot be certain whether your choice will be right or wrong.

You might try this method: Take a sheet of paper. Near the top draw a horizontal line.

On the left half put the word "Plus." On the right half the word "Minus." In the appropriate column list all the things that are positive and negative about your choices.

By listing the pluses and minuses at the bottom, you probably will have your answer to your problem. If this doesn't do it, try your gut feeling or network it, i.e., ask others for their advice.

A tried and true caveat is this: Do not, I repeat, *do not* lend money or sign as cosigner for a friend or relative because in the end you may lose the money. Don't do it out of love or friendship; you could lose either or both. You can blame me if the person wanting the loan asks you why you cannot help him or her. The result in due time will be that your friend or relative will still like and respect you.

More Decisions

After high school, if you plan to attend college, you must decide which ones to apply to and, if you are accepted to multiple colleges and/or universities, which to attend. These decisions are among the biggest investments you could ever make and, according to all available statistics, should pay off very well.

If you are having difficulty deciding what to do, ask yourself, "Who, what, when, where, why, how, and if?"

Later in life, buying a home could be your largest one-time investment, unless it would be to go into business. These investments are dependent on how you decide to invest your money. More decisions!

For most large transactions you are not expected to make decisions on the spot. Take a good look at the investment (problem), and do not be afraid to ask older and more experienced people for their advice. Then and only then should you make the final decision, either yes or no.

Sooner or later after you graduate, you will realize that somewhere, someplace you will need to research a book on " how to." It might be an encyclopedia or a highly technical magazine that explains in plain English the solution to a problem you want to solve. You may well need to consult such a source more than once in your lifetime. The more you do, the more knowledgeable you will become, and you will enjoy learning some of the things you missed in school or at home.

Finally, if your life is not turning out the way you expected, *stop, look,* and *listen!*

Review your life up to that moment. Take a good look at yourself while standing in front of a large mirror and ask yourself, no, tell yourself that up until now you consider yourself a failure. Or, if you are just not happy, ask yourself, "What do you plan to do about it?"

We are back to decisions, and this time you have to make them, as there is nothing guaranteed in life except death and taxes.

Good luck.

Chapter 8

Wills and Living Trusts

(Will Your Will Be Done?)

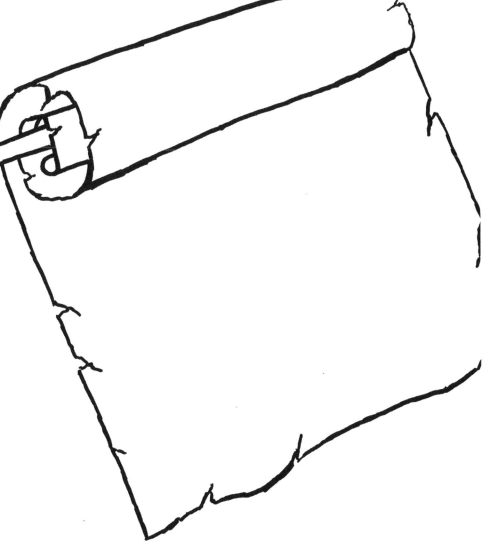

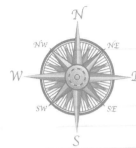

OVER YOUR LIFETIME you will hear many stories about wills or maybe no wills. Some wills have been made with much forethought. Others are done without much thinking ahead as to where the assets will go at the time of your demise.

Examples of disastrous endings are legendary and too numerous to mention. They are caused by poor advice or not thinking of possibilities that may occur in the future if your will or trust is not done properly.

Younger people make mistakes because of lack of experience or never having witnessed a death experience.

The next few pages will attest to what you should be aware of. Yes, we know you feel you are too young to have to go through this life experience, but we all do.

Some years ago, a wealthy Californian won a footnote in the law journals by writing a will on his nurse's petticoat. After the man died, the petticoat was hauled into court, and the instructions on it were carried out.

In another case, however, an eight-page will prepared by an experienced attorney triggered a bitter family battle. A man had left a sister "My property at the southeast corner of State and Madison Streets." Shortly before his death, though, the man had sold that particular parcel and bought a similar one across the street. Did he want his sister to have that instead?

The court decided that he did not—but no one really knows what he had in mind. How about you and your will?

#1 Hot Weather Special

John had thought about writing a will for years but never quite got around to it. One July afternoon he finally did. It was his wife's idea. They were flying to Europe the following day on their first vacation in years. "I guess you know what to put in it," John told the lawyer. "Something simple. Everything to my wife if I check out; everything to the kids if we go together. You run it through the typewriter, and I'll be back to sign it after I pick up the plane tickets."

The lawyer protested feebly, but he knew it was a lost cause. Fortunately, nothing did happen to John and his wife on the trip or in the years since. And that "Hot Weather Special" (which is what the legal profession calls them) has been serving as John's last will and testament ever since. The errors in it, and the trouble it would cause if probated, are many. To name a few: The executor, a non-resident of the state, would be disqualified from serving under the laws of the state. The will fails to mention a guardian to care for the young children if both John and his wife should die. The will makes no use of the tax-saving devices that are available.

The Moral: Simple wills are for simple people. If you have a business, any outside investments, and an estate of more than $600,000, that leaves you out.

#2 The Specific Problem

Smith had some firm ideas about who should get his property, and so he broke down his bequests in great detail: the Buick to brother Edward, the summer cottage to sister Nancy, the outboard motor and the Remington shotgun to Junior, all the jewelry to Aunt Min, and $10,000 in cash to the Republic Foundation from Phonetic Spelling. Mrs. Smith was to inherit the remainder, an amount of about $100,000 at the time the will was written.

Smith died last summer, in the fullness of his years, and his will was carried out—with some modifications. The Buick had long since been traded in for a Pontiac, so brother Edward received nothing. The jewelry for Aunt Min, worth $4,000 at the time of the bequest, had been augmented by recent purchases and was worth about $15,000 when she received it. Junior got the motor and the shotgun, and the Republic Foundation received the full $10,000. But, thanks to serious reverses in the investments, only about $25,000 remained for Mrs. Smith.

The Moral: Specific bequests are risky; use them with care, review them often. Generally, it's best to leave personal items to one trusted individual, say, your wife, with a separate letter of instructions on how they are to be distributed. For cash gifts, it's a good idea to include a percentage limitation, such as "$10,000 or 10 percent of my estate, whichever is less," to protect the last person in line.

#3 The Exhausted Executor

"I'd be honored to serve," said Bill when Dr. Walker asked him to be his executor. But like most amateurs at the job, Bill had no idea of what was involved. Since he was a lifelong friend, he naturally waived the usual executor's fee. That turned out to be an expensive economy for the estate after Dr. Walker died.

Bill's first problem came when he tried to dispose of the doctor's practice. Bill knew the lumber business cold, but he didn't have the foggiest notion of what a going dental practice was worth and how to begin to sell it. While he fenced with prospective buyers, patients drifted away, and the value of the practice dwindled.

After he finally sold the practice, at a fraction of its original value, other problems followed close behind. Among the tasks Bill had to perform: probate the will, take possession of all personal effects, collect the life insurance, investigate and pay all claims, manage or dispose of all property, file final income and estate tax returns, and then distribute the bequests.

The time this took was doing Bill's lumber business no good at all. So in the end he hired a lawyer and accountant to handle the details, with the estate picking up the tab. Still, as Bill is painfully aware, he remains personally liable for the assets in the estate and their ultimate distribution; though he doesn't say so aloud, Bill wishes his friend had honored someone else.

The Moral: Administering an estate is a job for professionals, so hire a pro to do it. If you want the personal touch in all decisions, you could name your wife or close friend to serve as co-trustee with the bank. In any case, the fees are the same and are set by state law.

#4 The Blessed Event

Youngblood made out his will shortly after he was married and left everything to his wife. He'd had two children since then and hasn't amended his will.

Lawyers warned him that in his state any children born after the will was signed would be entitled to a share of his estate. The Mrs. will use the money for the children's support, Youngblood figures, and that will even everything out. Why waste money drawing up another will?

Actually, he will waste far more money if he doesn't. Mrs. Youngblood can, indeed, use the children's bequest for their own support. But she'll have to be bonded and paying bond fees as long as the children remain minors. She'll have to submit reports to the court on what she spends and why. That means legal and accounting fees, and yards of the old red tape.

The Moral: When a will is drawn, it should specifically deal with each new addition to the family. If yours doesn't, be sure to amend if after each new addition to the family.

#5 The Little "Improvement"

Dr. Alterman willed $20,000 to Uncle Jerome. "Not much of a gift at all," the doctor explained, "when you consider that Jerome practically raised me after Dad passed on."

But Uncle Jerome reached his reward earlier—in another way. After the funeral, Dr. Alterman pondered over his will. The decent thing, he decided, would be to split the money between Uncle Jerry's two children. So Dr. Alterman took pen in hand, scratched out Jerry's name, and substituted the names of his two children. He initialed the change in the margin and returned the will to his safe deposit box.

The changes were meaningless, as a lawyer-friend subsequently explained to Dr. Alterman. At best, they'd be ignored, and the money would go into Uncle Jerry's estate—which was then being sued by a half-brother that Jerry hadn't seen in thirty years. At worst, a court might declare the entire will invalid.

The Moral: The only thing you should do with your will is sign it, fold it, and pack it away in a safe place. Amendments to a will must be executed with the same care and formality as the original document.

#6 The Wonderful Intention

"I want my eyes given the eye bank, and my body donated to medical science. Then I want my earthly remains cremated and buried with the simplest possible ceremony."

Those were the instructions Dr. Noble gave to his attorney, and the attorney dutifully wrote them into the will. Then the doctor packed it away in his safe deposit box.

When the time came, the deposit box was opened, and the will was read. That was just one week after Dr. Noble had been laid to rest in the fanciest funeral a zealous salesman could push onto the grief-stricken widow.

Other noble intentions in a will may not be carried out. For example, you can't give away jointly-owned property; it goes directly to the other joint owner. Your life insurance goes to the beneficiary named in your policies, no matter what you direct in your will. You generally can't give your entire estate to charity. And you can't completely disinherit your wife, whatever your motives might be.

The Moral: A will can do just so much. Check with your attorney on other steps you should take to have your wishes carried out.

#7 Stuck with the Tax

Mr. Gingerly had given a good deal of thought to the distribution of his estate, which was pretty sizable. He listed a number of specific gifts to relatives, friends, and charity. He left the balance, about $150,000, to Mrs. Gingerly. He figured that should be ample to care for her comfortably.

It might have been—if she had received all the money. But in listing his beneficiaries, Gingerly had forgotten a big one, the Treasury Department. Unless a will specifically provides where the tax money is to come from, it's subtracted from the share of the residual claimant—in this case, Mrs. Gingerly. So Mrs. Gingerly was stuck with the tax for the entire estate, plus all the expenses of administering and settling it. She would wind up with less than $100,000, which was a good deal less than the amount Gingerly had planned for her.

The Moral: Uncle Sam is waiting in the wings along with all your other beneficiaries; in fact, he's first in line. Plan for his share as carefully as for anyone else's.

#8 The March of Time

Mr. Block's will was a model of legal draftsmanship in its day. But that day was about twenty years ago. If he would ever review it (which he won't), he would be astounded at some of the things it contains.

The will gives one-quarter of his estate to each of his three children, John, Mary, and Rodney. John is a dentist now and earning more than Daddy ever did. Mary is happily married to a school teacher and is struggling to raise her own three children on a teacher's salary of $13,000 a year.

Rodney let one fortune slip away in lard and is now up to his nostrils in coffee in Columbia. Clearly, the children's need for money—and their ability to handle it—is not what it appeared when they were infants.

As for Mrs. Block's share, that's to be paid to her in the form of a lifetime income—$200 per month. That may have been adequate in 1973, but in 2008…?

If he had read further in his will, Block would have noticed that one of his witnesses had since died and the other had moved across the country. The executor of the will, the one entrusted with carrying out its provisions, was adjudged legally incompetent by the courts.

Of course, the will didn't make use of the tax-saving devices enacted in the last twenty years. A one-sentence change in the will, to take full advantage of the marital deduction, could save the estate thousands of tax dollars.

The Moral: Every couple of years, air your will out. Let your attorney or estate planning consultant have a look at it also.

Living Trusts

Simple Revocable Living Trust—As the trustee and creator of this trust, you will retain during your life the right to deal in the trust assets just as you would if you held the shares in your own name individually. You can revoke the trust at any time prior to your death, and the assets will revert to you. Holding securities under such a trust affords all the advantages and none of the disadvantages of joint tenancy, since property held under this trust will automatically be transferred to your named beneficiary upon your death in exactly the same fashion as property held in joint names with the right of survivorship.

Level Payment Living Trust—Under this trust you also act as trustee for the remainder of your life, retaining the right to deal in the trust assets as you see fit or to revoke the trust at any time. However, upon your death, the trust continues in the hands of a successor trustee. Rather than receiving an outright distribution of the trust assets, your beneficiary will receive monthly fixed or quarterly payments from the trust. This trust has appealed to many investors who wish to provide regular payments for continued support of their beneficiaries. Discretionary powers can be given to the new trustee so that additional payments can be made from the principle if needed.

Marital Trust—Here again you have complete control of the trust during your lifetime, and the trust will continue under a successor trustee upon your death. Under this trust you leave your wife the right to receive the income from all the trust assets, but you give her the right to dispose of only one-half of it by her will. The other half goes upon her death to the persons you designate. By this means, you have the maximum benefit of the martial deduction for your estate, and your wife's taxable estate will be reduced to a minimum.

When a person sets up a trust, he transfers property from his own name to a trustee (either himself or another person).

Thereafter, the trustee has legal title to the property and must administer it according to the terms of the trust.

A "living trust" means a trust created during one's lifetime, as opposed to a trust created by the terms of a will. Such a trust will be completely revocable during the lifetime of the creator, who will serve as trustee during that period, and, for practical purposes, becomes operative only upon the death of the creator.

Avoid Delay and Expense

Although a will is perhaps the most conventional means of providing for the disposition of one's property, it has disadvantages that are not generally recognized.

Property passing under a will is subject to the jurisdiction of the probate court. The final settlement of an estate under a will requires, among other things, that the will be proved a valid document, an executor be appointed, claims of creditors be met, various accountings be made to the court, and finally, that the executor be officially discharged. All these steps involve delay and expense. The expense alone may often amount to 5 or even 10 percent or more of the assets passing under a will, and the minimum delay is usually fifteen months.

A revocable living trust created during one's lifetime can completely eliminate the delay and expense usually associated with the settling of an estate.

Living Will Declaration

Declaration made this _____ day of _____ (month, year), I, _____, being at least eighteen (18) years old and of sound mind, willfully and voluntarily make known my desires that my dying shall not be artificially prolonged under the circumstances set forth below, and I declare:

If at any time I have an incurable injury, disease, or illness certified in writing to be a terminal condition by my attending physician, and my attending physician has determined that my death will occur within a short period of time, and the use of life-prolonging procedures would serve only to artificially prolong the dying process, I direct that such procedures be withheld or withdrawn, and that I be permitted to die naturally with only the provision of appropriate nutrition and hydration and the administration of medication and the performance of any medical procedure necessary to provide me with comfort care or to alleviate pain.

In the absence of my ability to give directions regarding the use of life-prolonging procedures, it is my intention that this declaration be honored by my family and physician as the final expression of my legal right to refuse medical or surgical treatment and accept the consequences of the refusal.

I understand the full import of this declaration.

Signed _____   _____
                                                                              (City, County, and State of Residence)

The declarer has been personally known to me, and I believe (him/her) to be of sound mind. I did not sign the declarer's signature above or at the direction of the declarer. I am not a parent, spouse, or child of the declarer. I am not entitled to any part of the declarer's estate or directly financially responsible for the declarer's medical care. I am competent and at least eighteen (18) years old.

Witness _____ Date _____

Witness _____ Date _____

Chapter 9
The Good Life

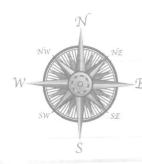

EVERYONE WANTS TO have the good life, but very few of us really get it. What are the reasons some of us are healthy and some of us are always ill? You may already have read enough health books to keep you well for a lifetime. The question is, though: Have you followed the suggestions given to you by your doctor and/or the magazines and books you have read?

Statistics show that over half of the prescriptions given by doctors are never filled and most likely a good share of the pills purchased are never taken as prescribed. Keep in mind that your body is like a fine-tuned machine. Use it that way; keep it that way. You don't put cheap gas in your car, so why would you put cheap items not good for your health in your beautiful body?

My rule is *everything in moderation*. That means eating, drinking, and sleeping. Sure, everyone cheats from time to time, but as a daily affair, no. When I mail a letter, I generally put the initials EIM after my name. When people ask me what it means, I explain what it means and how I follow my own rules.

Every day I walk three or four miles and sometimes more. There was a time when I jogged, but seeing and hearing about all the knee operations, I decided to take the easy way out. It is fun; it is exhilarating; it helps keep my weight in control; it is good for my body; and I get to meet some very nice people.

In addition to walking, daily body exercise (ten minutes per day) results in better coordination, less chance of falling, and all-around good muscle tone. So, set up your own rules and then follow them.

Each day, keep in mind three things:

ATTITUDE, ATTITUDE and ATTITUDE!

Expressions and Other Sayings

- Nothing happens until a sale is made.

- Always remember: "There is no free lunch."

- Expenses rise to meet income.

- Growing old is mandatory; growing up is optional.

- Work hard, but also work smart.

- If the price is a dream, then the service/support will be a nightmare.

- New technology is always priced just before your budget.

- An affordable notebook is a black-and-white notebook.

- Page one of an attorney's bible is: "Don't let the heirs loot the estate."

- Page one of the banker's bible is: "Convert all assets to cash."

- When they say, "It's not the money," it's the money.

- If you have to eat crow, eat it while it is still warm; it tastes better that way.

- Your first loss is your easiest loss. Don't ever forget that. (This is the best advice anyone can give you.)

- The general got on his horse and rode off in all directions.

- (Caveat: Don't be like the general.)

- No one is listening until you make a mistake.

- Always remember: You're unique, just like everyone else.

- It is far more impressive when others discover your good qualities without your help. If you think nobody cares whether you're alive, try missing a couple of car payments.

- Before you criticize someone, you should walk a mile in that person's shoes. That way, when you criticize the person, you're a mile away and you have his or her shoes.

- If you lend someone $20 and never see that person again, it was probably worth it.

- If you tell the truth, you don't have to remember anything.

- The quickest way to double your money is to fold it in half and put it back in your pocket.

- Generally speaking, you aren't learning much when your mouth is moving. Experience is something you don't get until just after you need it.

- We are the way we are because that is just the way we want to be.

—Earl Nightengale

Golden Rules for Living

If you open it, close it.

If you turn it on, turn it off.

If you unlock it, lock it up.

If you break it, admit it.

If you can't fix it, call in someone who can.

If you borrow it, return it.

If you value it, take care of it.

If you make a mess, clean it up.

If you move it, put it back.

If it belongs to someone else, get permission to use it.

If you don't know how to operate it, leave it alone.

If it's none of your business, don't ask questions.

—Author Unknown

One Day at a Time

Whatever the goals you're pursuing,
No matter how rugged the climb,
You're certain to get there
By trying your best,
And taking one day at a time.
"Forever" is hard to imagine,
"The future" may seem far away,
But every new dawn
Brings a wonderful chance,
To do what you can day by day.

How to Live to Be One Hundred and Feel Young All the Way

For five years, my colleagues and I studied more than 150 people age one hundred and older to learn their survival secrets.

Rather than being plagued by chronic and acute illnesses typically associated with old age, the people we studied were vibrant and healthy the vast majority of their lives. And they were completely aware of everything going on around them.

We also learned that participants shared specific habits started earlier in their lives that helped them live long lives and minimize poor health and minor disabilities in their later years.

Lighten Your Emotional Loads: Every person we studied tested low levels of neuroticism—unhealthful feelings of extreme anger, anxiety, or sadness.

These feelings can disturb heart beats, reduce immune functioning, and even accelerate the aging process. The people in our group all had the ability to easily shed emotional stress, tended to be calm and collected during crises, and easily adapted to changes in their environments.

Key: Although you may not be able to change your personality, through practice you can change the way you respond to life stresses. One way to respond is by learning to let go of what can't be changed. Stress-reduction techniques, such as daily meditation and deep-breathing exercises, are especially helpful.

What to Do: Once a day, take a conscious "stress-buster" break—even if you don't feel especially stressed. Close your eyes, focus only on the sounds of your breathing, and slowly exhale and inhale. Learning to adapt to changing situations is another common characteristic among our winning one-hundred-year-olds.

But adaptability entails more than responding to outside forces. Equally important is the ability to take charge of life situations.

The next time you're faced with a difficult situation, write down the things you can control in one column and those you can't in the other. List all the action steps you can take to address items listed in the "can control" column. Keep a running log of what worked and what didn't so you can refer to it next time.

Eat and Drink in Moderation: We couldn't find any specific foods or nutrients that all the people we studied consumed. But moderation appeared to be important. Remarkably, about 80 percent of the people said that their current weight was close to what they weighed their entire adult life.

Many of the people in the study ate moderate amounts of high-fat foods throughout their lives, but they got away with it because of their genes. The majority of us can't afford such indulgences. We especially need to avoid trans-fatty acids—the hydrogenated fats commonly found in cookies, biscuits, and margarine. Trans-fatty acids are not only high in calories—they can also significantly increase LDL ("bad") cholesterol and reduce HDL ("good") cholesterol, raising the risk for heart disease. These people also tended to keep their sugar intake to a minimum. This is especially relevant since large amounts of dietary sugar can lead to obesity and, consequently, cause diabetes.

Key: Eat smaller meals more often to reduce cravings. Restrict alcohol intake to no more than two to four ounces a day. Most of the people in our group did not consume alcohol. That helped keep their blood sugar under control.

Consciously Challenge Your Brain: Cognitive capacity is one of the most critical factors in reaching old, old age. Interestingly, even though senility and aging have long been thought to go hand in hand, the people in our group maintained most of their mental abilities and personalities.

Reason: While brain deterioration is an inevitable part of aging, an important means of overcoming mental decline is the growth of new dendrites. These are branchlike extensions between nerve cells that allow the exchange of chemical and electrical information. The formation of these networks creates a reserve that distributes responsibility for certain functions across areas of the brain. This distribution increases the ability to compensate for cell loss or destruction that results from disease.

Throughout their lives, every person in our group engaged in some sort of multidimensional activity that exercised different parts of their brains.

Best Activities: Several people were working on or had completed their autobiographies when we first met them. This form of writing stimulates the mind by forcing the integration of current beliefs with past experiences.

Another brain-boosting activity is playing a musical instrument. It requires simultaneous reading, listening, memorizing, and using manual skills. It produces multiple benefits for the brain, including boosting its ability to resist trauma and illness. Music has also been shown to reduce the negative impacts of stress. Other effective activities include painting and learning new languages.

Stay in Touch with Friends and Make New Ones: Despite the fact that most people in our group had outlived their spouses and dearest friends, they never seemed to be alone and maintained social contacts with people of all ages.

The ability to attract people to you as you age is a critical survival factor. And a social network ensures help in times of need.

Regular social contact can also lower potentially harmful hormones that are released by the body during stressful situations.

Positive outlook and a sense of humor tend to play an important role in these people's personal magnetism.

Also, make a commitment to volunteer in the community, participate in clubs and other member oriented activities, move closer to family members or simply call more people more often. Having regular human contact may seem small, but it helps build important bridges that may be absent or have lapsed to create a social web for the future.

Make Daily Exercise a Must: The merits of regular exercise in terms of preventing or delaying chronic disease are well known. It also appears that activities that prevent significant muscle loss can have an impact on longevity.

Best Activities: Most of the centenarians we studied spent years living on the second or third floor of their buildings. So they climbed the stairs everyday. Like stair climbing, walking also improves balance and leg strength. That decreases the risk of falls and, consequently, debilitation and death among the elderly.

—Thomas T. Perls, MD, Harvard Med.

Poems, Sayings, and Other Expressions

Three Things

Three things in life that, once gone, never come back:

Time *Words* *Opportunity*

Three things in life that may never be lost

Peace *Hope* *Charity*

Three things in life that are most valuable:

Love *Self-confidence* *Friends*

Three things in life that are never certain:

Dreams *Success* *Fortune*

Three things that make a successful person:

Hard work *Sincerity* *Commitment*

Three things in life that can destroy a successful person:

Alcohol *Pride* *Anger*

Three things in life you should strive for:

Knowledge *Continuing education* *Empathy*

—Author Unknown

The Success Family

The father of success is work;
The mother of success is ambition;
The oldest son is common sense.

Some of the other boys are—
Perseverance, Honesty, Thoroughness,
Foresight, Enthusiasm, and Cooperation.

The oldest sister is Character;
Some of her sisters are—
Cheerfulness, Loyalty, Care,
Courtesy, Economy, Sincerity,
and the baby is Opportunity.
Get acquainted with the old man
and you will be able to get along
pretty well with the rest of the family.

—Author Unknown

Note: I have carried a copy of this for almost fifty years.

Don't Quit

When things go wrong, as they sometimes will,
When the road you're trudging seems all up hill,
When the funds are low and the debts are high,
And you want to smile but you have to sigh,
When care is pressing you down a bit,
Rest, if you must—but don't you quit.

Life is queer with its twists and turns,
As every one of us sometimes learns,
And many a failure turns about,
When he might of won had he stuck it out;
Don't give up, though the pace may seem slow,
You might succeed with another blow.

Often the goal is nearer than it seems to the faint and fal-
tering, often the struggler has given up when they might
have captured the victor's cup.

As they learned too late, when the night slipped down,
How close they were to the golden crown.

Success is failure turned inside out, the silver tint of the
clouds of doubt, and you can never tell how close you are,
It may be near when it seems afar;
So stick to the fight when you're hardest hit
It's when things seem worst that you mustn't quit.
                                        —Author Unknown

Read it, study it, remember it.

Frank's Pithy Bits That You Can Use Over the Balance of Your Life

- You can never make a second first impression.

- No matter how carefully you move it, dump it, or compact it, one thing is certain: You know you are going to run out of sky.

- It takes longer than expected.

- It costs more than anticipated.

- The competition is smarter than you think.

- Failure to take advantage of new technology in your field will tell on your bottom line.

Ninety-Nine Rules of Project Schedules

The first ninety percent of the task takes ninety percent of the time, and the other ten percent take the other ninety percent.

Rule of Accuracy:

When working toward the solution of a problem, it always helps you if you know the answer.

Sattinger's Law:

It works better if you plug it in.

Mesimen's Law:

There never is time to do it right, but always time to do it over.

Zymurgy's First Law of System Dynamics:

Once you open a can of worms, the only way you can re-can them is to use a larger can.

John's Collateral Corollary:

In order to get a loan you must first prove you don't need it.

Gilb's Laws of Reliability:

Any system that depends on human reliability is unreliable.

Lowry's Law:

If it jams, force it; if it breaks, it needed replacing anyway.

Boren's First Law:

When in doubt, mumble.

Brook's Law:

Adding manpower to a late software project makes it later.

Cann's Axiom:

> *When all else fails, read the instructions.*

Ginsberg's Theorem:

> *You can't win.*
>
> *You can't break even.*
>
> *You can't even quit the game.*

Gordon's First Law:

> *If a research project is not worth doing at all, it is not worth doing well.*

Harvard Law:

> *Under the most rigorously controlled conditions of pressure, temperature, volume, humidity, and other variables, the organism will do as it damn well pleases.*

Laws of Computer Programming:

> *Any given program, when running, is obsolete.*
>
> *Any given program costs more and takes longer.*
>
> *If a program is useful, it will have to be changed.*
>
> *If a program is useless, it will have to be documented.*
>
> *The value of a program is proportional to the weight of its output.*

Johnson-Laird's Law:

> *Toothache tends to start on Saturday night.*

The Golden Rule of Arts and Sciences:

> *Whoever has the gold makes the rules.*

—Bexdata, Corliss Beck

Take Time for Your Mom

Today is my mother's birthday. For the first time since I was a little girl, I cannot give her a gift.

After I married, we lived only a few miles apart. I always managed to run in and drop off a present I had picked up at the last minute. Sometimes I didn't even wait long enough to have it gift wrapped.

No matter what it was, she'd smile and say "Thank you!" Then I'd head for the door and she would sigh, "I wish you could sit down and visit for a little while. You are always in such a hurry."

My stock answer was, "I wish I could, Mom, and I will, one of these days. We'll have a really good visit, but today, I have so many things to do, I must get going." For the life of me, I can't remember what I was doing that was so important, but I was always running. "One of these days" will never come because Mom passed away last week. For the very first time in her wonderful, unselfish life, she was the one who didn't have time for me. She had a massive heart attack and went so fast, I'm not sure she heard me say, "I love you, MOM."

Time has a sneaky way of slipping away. We all get so involved in our own little worlds, and before you know it, the tomorrows are yesterdays. If I can encourage just one person to stop, no matter how busy, and find an hour to visit his or her mother, it will be the best gift I could give my mom.

—Ann Landers

Thank Your Mom Before It's Too Late

When you came into the world, she held you in her arms.
You thanked her by wailing in her arms. You thanked her by wailing like a
   banshee.

When you were 1 year old, she fed you and bathed you.
You thanked her by crying all night long.

When you were 2 years old, she taught you to walk.
You thanked her by running away when she called.

When you were 3 years old, she made all your meals with love.
You thanked her by tossing your plate on the floor.

When you were 4 years old, she gave you some crayons.
You thanked her by coloring the dining room table.

When you were 5 years old, she dressed you for the holidays.
You thanked her by plopping into the nearest pile of mud.

When you were 6 years old, she walked you to school.
You thanked her by screaming, *"I'm not going!"*

When you were 7 years old, she bought you a baseball.
You thanked her by throwing it through the next-door-neighbor's window.

When you were 8 years old, she handed you an ice cream.
You thanked her by dripping it all over your lap.

When you were 9 years old, she paid for piano lessons.
You thanked her by never even bothering to practice.

When you were 10 years old, she drove you all day, from soccer to gymnastics
   to one birthday party after another.
You thanked her by jumping out of the car and never looking back.

When you were 11 years old, she took you and your friends to the movies.
You thanked her by asking to sit in a different row.

When you were 12 years old, she warned you not to watch certain TV shows.
You thanked her by waiting until she left the house.

Those teenage years

When you were 13, she suggested a haircut that was becoming.
You thanked her by telling her she had no taste.

When you were 14, she paid for a month away at summer camp.
You thanked her by forgetting to write a single letter.

When you were 15, she came home from work, looking for a hug.
You thanked her by having your bedroom door locked.

When you were 16, she taught you how to drive her car.
You thanked her by taking it every chance you could.

When you were 17, she was expecting an important call.
You thanked her by being on the phone all night.

When you were 18, she cried at your high school graduation.
You thanked her by staying out partying until dawn.

Growing old and gray

When you were 19, she paid for your college tuition, drove you to campus,
  carried your bags.
You thanked her by saying good-bye outside the dorm so you wouldn't be
  embarrassed in front of your friends.

When you were 20, she asked whether you were seeing anyone.
You thanked her by saying, "It's none of your business."

When you were 21, she suggested certain careers for your future.
You thanked her by saying, "I don't want to be like you."

When you were 22, she hugged you at your college graduation.
You thanked her by asking whether she could pay for a trip to Europe.

When you were 23, she gave you furniture for your first apartment.
You thanked her by telling your friends it was ugly.

When you were 24, she met your fiancée and asked about your plans for the future.
You thanked her by glaring and growling, "Muuhh-ther, please!"

When you were 25, she helped to pay for your wedding, and she cried and told you how deeply she loved you.
You thanked her by moving halfway across the country.

When you were 30, she called with some advice on the baby.
You thanked her by telling her, "Things are different now."

When you were 40, she called to remind you of a relative's birthday.
You thanked her by saying you were "really busy right now."

When you were 50, she fell ill and needed you to take care of her.
You thanked her by reading about the burden parents become to their children. And then, one day she quietly died.

And everything you never did came crashing down like thunder.

Each day she lives should be Mother's Day. And you wonder how you'll ever repay all the loving, feeding, bathing, teaching, driving, guiding, and caring you've received.

Well, as your mother might say:

You can start by saying, *"thank you."*

—Author Unknown

Because I Said So, and Other Motherisms

On Sunday, we'll celebrate Mother's Day. I asked colleagues, friends, and relatives to come up with their favorite "motherisms." Here are just a few:

On discipline: "Don't make me have to come back there."

On making you wear a shirt with sleeves that are too short: "If you roll them up, who can tell?"

On buying shoes that are slightly too big: "When you're wearing heavy socks, they will fit just fine."

On keeping the old shoes: "You can use the new pair as your school shoes and kick around the house in the others."

On wearing hand-me-downs: "Your brother only wore these once or twice."

Upon asking her for money: "Do I look like a bank?" which evolved into, "Do I look like a cash station?"

Upon asking her opinion: "Do what you want. You will anyway."

On watching a son gulp down a meal: "What girl is going to want to sit and watch you eat like that?"

On watching a daughter gulp down a meal: "What boy is going to want to sit and watch you eat like that?"

Upon passing a lighted room: "Am I the only one in this house who knows how to turn off a light?"

Upon passing a bathroom: "Am I the only one who knows how to change the toilet paper roll?"

On challenging her intelligence: "You must think I'm a fool." "I wasn't born yesterday, you know." "I've been where you're trying to go."

On challenging your intelligence: "I bet you think you're so smart."

On obedience: "While you're living here, you'll dance to my music."

On dancing to music: "Don't shake your butt like that in my house."

On wearing too much makeup: "You're not leaving this house looking like a clown."

On burned toast: "Just scrape it off."

On swallowing your pride: "Just swallow fast."

On forgetfulness: "You'd forget your head if it weren't attached to you."

On being nosy: "Stay out of grown folks' business."

On self-reliance: "God helps those who help themselves." "If your friends jump into Lake Michigan, I suppose you'd follow too, huh?" (Note: The body of water can change to read: the Mississippi, the Danube, etc., depending on one's geography.)

On remaining chaste: "Why buy the cow when the milk is free?" "Don't you go out there and bring me no hereafters."

On running away: "You can leave, but take only the things you came here with." "Hey, I'll pack your clothes and send them to you later."

Idle and politically incorrect threats: The Bill Cosby-esque, "I brought you into this world; I'll take you out." "I'll knock you into next Tuesday."

On reprimanding the neighbor child: "Does your mama let you do that at your home?"

A mother's curse: "I hope someday you'll have children just like you." "I hope I live long enough to see your children treat you the way you treat me."

On that trip called guilt: "All I want is a few kind words." "Is that too much to ask?" "Don't worry about me, I'll be all right." "Are you proud of yourself?" "I endured many hours of labor, and you can't do what I ask?" "Just who do you think you are?" "The poor children in Haiti would kill to have what you have." "A mother is the last to know." "I never made my mother cry."

Her pearls of wisdom: "There's always free cheese in a mouse trap." "You'll be an adult forever; what's your hurry?" "Give folks their flowers while they're living." "Happiness is a direction, not a place." "You think that's heartache? Just keep on living." "Every knockdown is a boost." "Just remember, I love you no matter what."

—Dawn Turner Trice, *Chicago Tribune*

The Subtitle of This Book Is "What Your Parents and Teachers Did Not Teach You in School"— These Are Some of the Things My Mother Did Teach Me

My mother taught me *to appreciate a job well done*: "If you're going to kill each other, do it outside—I just finished cleaning!"

My mother taught me *religion*: "You better pray that will come out of the carpet."

My mother taught me about *time travel*: "If you don't straighten up, I'm going to knock you into the middle of next week!"

My mother taught me *logic*: "Because I said so, that's why."

My mother taught me *foresight*: "Make sure you wear clean underwear, in case you're in an accident."

My mother taught me *irony*: "Keep laughing and I'll give you something to cry about."

My mother taught me about the science of *osmosis*: "Shut your mouth and eat your supper!"

My mother taught me *contortionism*: "Will you look at the dirt on the back of your neck!"

My mother taught me about *stamina*: "You'll sit there 'til all that spinach is finished."

My mother taught me about *weather*: "It looks as if a tornado swept through your room."

My mother taught me how to solve *physics problems*: "If I yelled because I saw a meteor coming toward you, would you listen then?"

My mother taught me about *hypocrisy*: "If I've told you once, I've told you a million times—Don't exaggerate!!!"

My mother taught me *the circle of life*: "I brought you into this world, and I can take you out."

My mother taught me about *behavior modification*: "Stop acting like your father!"

My mother taught me about *envy*: "There are millions of less fortunate children in this world who don't have wonderful parents like you do!"

—Author Unknown

In the Eighty-Seven Years of My Life

I've learned—

> *That regardless of how hot and steamy a relationship is at first, the passion fades and there had better be something else to take its place.*

I've learned—

> *That you cannot make someone love you. All you can do is be someone who can be loved. The rest is up to the other person.*

I've learned—

> *That no matter how much I care, some people just don't care back.*

I've learned—

> *That it takes years to build up trust and only seconds to destroy it.*

I've learned—

> *That it's not what you have in your life but who you have in your life that counts.*

I've learned—

> *That you can get by on charm for about fifteen minutes. After that, you'd better know something.*

I've learned—

> *That you shouldn't compare yourself to the best others can do.*

I've learned—

> *That you can do something in an instant that will give you heartache for life.*

I've learned—

> *That it's taking me a long time to become the person I want to be.*

I've learned—

> *That you should always leave loved ones with loving words. It may be the last time you see them.*

I've learned—

That you can keep going long after you can't.

I've learned—

That we are responsible for what we do, no matter how we feel.

I've learned—

That either you control your attitude or it controls you.

I've learned—

That heroes are the people who do what has to be done when it needs to be done, regardless of the consequences.

I've learned—

That money is a lousy way of keeping score.

I've learned—

That my best friend and I can do anything or nothing and have the best time.

I've learned—

That sometimes the people you expect to kick you when you're down will be the ones to help you get back up.

I've learned—

That sometimes when I'm angry I have the right to be angry, but that doesn't give me the right to be cruel.

I've learned—

That true friendship continues to grow, even over the longest distance. Same goes for true love.

I've learned—

That just because people don't love you the way you want them to doesn't mean they don't love you with all they have.

I've learned—

> *That maturity has more to do with what types of experiences you've had and what you've learned from them and less to do with how many birthdays you've celebrated.*

I've learned—

> *That you should never tell children their dreams are unlikely or outlandish. Few things are more humiliating, and what a tragedy it would be if they believed it.*

I've learned—

> *That your family won't always be there for you. It may seem funny, but people you aren't related to can take care of you and love you and teach you to trust people again. Families aren't biological.*

I've learned—

> *That no matter how good friends are, they're going to hurt you every once in a while, and you must forgive them for that.*

I've learned—

> *That it isn't always enough to be forgiven by others. Sometimes you have to learn to forgive yourself.*

I've learned—

> *That no matter how bad your heart is broken the world doesn't stop for your grief.*

I've learned—

> *That our background and circumstances may have influenced who we are, but we are responsible for whom we become.*

I've learned—

> *That just because two people argue, it doesn't mean they don't love each other. And just because they don't argue, it doesn't mean they do.*

I've learned—

> *That we don't have to change friends if we understand that friends change.*

I've learned—

> *That you shouldn't be so eager to find out a secret. It could change your life forever.*

I've learned—

> *That two people can look at the exact same thing and see something totally different.*

I've learned—

> *That no matter how you try to protect your children, they will eventually get hurt, and you will also get hurt in the process.*

I've learned—

> *That your life can be changed in a matter of hours by people who don't even know you.*

I've learned—

> *That even when you think you have no more to give, when a friend cries out to you, you will find the strength to help.*

I've learned—

> *That credentials on the wall do not make you a decent human being.*

I've learned—

> *That the people you care about most in life are taken from you too soon.*

I've learned—

> *That it's hard to determine where to draw the line between being nice and not hurting people's feelings and standing up for what you believe.*

—My thanks to the Internet

Looking Back…
Comments that might have been made in the year 1957:

"I'll tell you one thing, if things keep going the way they are, it's going to be impossible to buy a week's groceries for $20."

"Have you seen the new cars coming out next year? It won't be long when $5,000 will only buy a used one."

"If cigarettes keep going up in price, I'm going to quit. A quarter a pack is ridiculous."

"Did you hear the post office is thinking about charging a dime just to mail a letter?"

"If they raise the minimum wage to $1, nobody will be able to hire outside help at the store."

"When I first started driving, who would have thought gas would someday cost 29 cents a gallon. Guess we'd be better off leaving the car in the garage."

"Kids today are impossible. Those ducktail haircuts make it impossible to stay groomed. Next thing you know, boys will be wearing their hair as long as girls."

"I'm afraid to send my kids to the movies anymore. Ever since they let Clark Gable get by with saying 'damn' in *Gone With the Wind*, it seems every new movie has either 'hell' or 'damn' in it."

"I read the other day that some scientist thinks it's possible to put a man on the moon by the end of the century. They even have some fellows they call astronauts preparing for it down in Texas."

"Did you see where some baseball player just signed a contract for $75,000 a year just to play ball? It wouldn't surprise me if someday that they will be making more than the President."

"I never thought I'd see the day all our kitchen appliances would be electric. They are even making electric typewriters now."

"It's too bad things are so tough nowadays. I see where a few married women have to work to make ends meet."

"It won't be long before young couples are going to have to hire someone to watch their kids so they can both work."

"Marriage doesn't mean a thing anymore; those Hollywood stars seem to be getting divorces at the drop of a hat."

"I'm just afraid the Volkswagen car is going to open the door to a whole lot of foreign business."

"Thank goodness I won't live to see the day when the government takes half our income in taxes. I sometimes wonder whether we are electing the best people to Congress."

"The drive-in restaurant is convenient in nice weather, but I seriously doubt they will ever catch up."

"There is no sense in going to Lincoln or Omaha anymore for a weekend. It costs nearly $15 a night to stay in a hotel."

"No one can afford to be sick anymore: $35 a day in the hospital is too rich for my blood."

"Have you seen those new Chevy Bel Airs with the big fins? Nobody is gonna want one of those."

The Station

Tucked away in our subconscious is an idyllic vision. We see ourselves on a long trip that spans the continent. We are traveling by train. Out the windows we drink in the passing scenes of cars on nearby highways, of children waving at a crossing, of cattle grazing on a distant hillside, of smoke pouring from a power plant, of row upon row of corn and wheat, of flatland and valleys, of mountains and rolling hillsides, of city skylines and village halls.

But, uppermost in our minds is the final destination. Bands will be playing and flags waving. Once we get there, our dreams will come true, and the pieces of our lives will fit together like a jigsaw puzzle. How restless we pace the aisles, damning the minutes for loitering—waiting, waiting, waiting for the station.

"When we reach the station, that will be it!" we cry.

"When I'm eighteen."

"When I buy a new 450SL Mercedes-Benz."

"When I put the last kid through college."

"When I have paid off the mortgage."

"When I get a promotion."

"When I reach the age of retirement, I shall live happily ever after."

Sooner or later we must realize that there is no station, no one place to arrive at once and for all. The true joy of life is the trip. The station is only a dream. It constantly outdistances us.

"Relish the moment" is a good motto, especially when coupled with Psalms 118:24: "This is the day which the Lord hath made; we will rejoice and be glad in it." It isn't the burdens of today that drive men mad. Regret and fear are twin thieves who rob us of today. So stop pacing the aisles and counting the miles. Instead, climb more mountains, eat more ice cream, go barefoot more often, swim more rivers, watch more sunsets, laugh more, cry less.

Life must be lived as we go along. The station will come soon enough.

—Robert Hastings

My Friend

Around the corner I have a friend
in this great town that has no end,
yet days go by and weeks rush on,
and ere I know it, a year has gone,
and I never see my old friend's face,
for life is a swift and terrible race.

He knows I like him just as well, as in
days when I rang his bell and he rang mine.

We were younger then, and now we are busy
and tired men—tired with playing a
foolish game, tired with trying to find a name.

"Tomorrow," I say, "I'll call on him,"
just to show I'm thinking of him—but
tomorrow comes and tomorrow goes, and
the distance between us grows and grows.

Around the corner, yet miles away!
comes this message, "Here's a telegram, sir"
JIM DIED TODAY

And that's what we get and deserve in the end
around the corner—a vanished friend...
                                        —Charles Hanson Towne

The Dash

I read of a man who stood to speak at the funeral of a friend, he referred to the dates on her tombstone from the beginning…to the end.

He noted that first came the date of her birth and spoke of the following date with tears, but he said what mattered most of all was the dash between those years.

For that dash represents all of the time that she spent alive on earth…and now only those who loved her know what that little line is worth.

For it matters not, how much we own: the cars…the house…the cash. What matters most is how we live and love and how we spend our dash.

So think about this long and hard…are there things you'd like to change? for you never know how much time is left.

(You could be at "dash mid-range.")

If we could just slow down enough to consider what's true and real, and always try to understand the way other people feel.

And be less quick to anger, and show appreciation more and love the people in our lives like we have never loved before.

If we treat each other with respect, and more often wear a smile…remembering that this special dash might only last a while.

So, when your eulogy's being read with your life's actions to rehash, would you be proud of the things they say about how you spent your dash?

—Linda Ellis

I Wonder

What would I do if I knew today was my last day on earth?

I wonder! Would I try to put right all the hurts and the wrongs, the many mistakes I've made? Would I try to put the sunshine back into the smiles I've seen fade?

What would I say if I knew today was my last day on earth? I wonder!

Would I say to my family, I've loved you so much, the joys, the sorrows, the sharing.

What would the world say about me tomorrow if this was my last day on earth?

I wonder!

Would it remember someone who tried to do right, although sometimes demanding and cross? Would it miss me a bit, this world that I love and feel a real sense of loss?

Each one must live each day that is given and be ready to pay for each blunder.

But what would I do if I knew today was my last day on earth?

I wonder!

Courtesy: M. Benninghoff and M. Leddy

Miss Me—But Let Me Go

*When I come to the end of the road
and the sun has set for me,
I want no rites in a gloom filled room
why cry for a soul set free?*

*Miss me a little—but not for long
and not with your head bowed low;
remember the love that we once shared;
miss me—but let me go.*

*For this is a journey that all must take
and each must go alone;
it's all part of the Master's plan,
a step on the road home.*

*When you are lonely and sick of heart,
go to friends that we know
and bury your sorrows in doing good deeds;
miss me—but let me go.*

—Leroy Olson

Beauty

Beautiful are the youth
whose rich emotions flash and burn,
whose lithe bodies
filled with energy and grace
sway in their happy
dance of life;

And beautiful likewise
are the mature
who have learned
compassion and patience,
charity and wisdom,
though they be rarer far
than beautiful youth.

But most beautiful and most rare
is the gracious old age
which has drawn from life
the skill to take varied strands;
the harsh advance of age,
the pang of grief,
the passing of dear friends,
the loss of strength,
and with fresh insight
weave them into
a rich and gracious pattern all of its own.

This is the greatest skill of all,
to take the bitter with the sweet
and make it beautiful;
to take the whole of life in all its moods,
its strengths and weaknesses,
and of the whole
make one great
and celestial harmony.

—Robert Terry Weston

New Friends and Old Friends

Make new friends, but keep the old;
those are silver, these are gold.
new-made friendships, like new wine,
age will mellow and refine
friendships that have stood the test...
time and change—are surely best;

Brow may wrinkle, hair grow gray;
friendship never knows decay
for 'mid old friends, tried and true,
once more we our youth renew.

But old friends, alas! may die
new friends must their place supply.
cherish friendship in your breast –
new is good, but old is best;
make new friends, but keep the old;
those are silver, these are gold.

—Joseph Parry

Eighty Today, Dear Lord

Eighty today, dear Lord, I am eighty, and there's much I haven't done. I hope, dear Lord, you'll let me live until I'm 81.

Because I haven't finished all I want to do, would you please let me stay awhile, until I'm 82?

So many places I want to go, so much I want to see. Do you think you could manage to make it 83?

Many things I may have done, but there's so much left in store, I'd like it very much to live to 84.

And if by then, I'm still alive, then I'd like to stay to 85.

The world is changing very fast, so I'd really like to stick and see what happens to the world when I'm 86.

I know, dear Lord, it's a lot to ask, and it will be nice in heaven, but I'd really like to stay around until I'm 87.

I know by then I won't be fast, and sometimes, I'll be late, but it would be oh-so-pleasant to be around at 88.

I will have seen so many things and had a wonderful time, so I'm sure that I'll be willing to leave at 89.

(Well, maybe.)

—Author Unknown

Take Time to Live

We should all take time to live
before each day goes rushing by,
time to search for deeper meanings
and to give our dreams a try.

Time for laughter, time for music
time for flowers, trees and birds.
time to look for new ideas
and to put our thoughts in words.

Time for talking to our neighbors
time to search the mind and heart.
Time alone—to help us bring
our best to every day we start.

—Author Unknown

Why Worry About Tomorrow

Why worry about tomorrow
and the rising of the Sun,
or anguish over past mistakes
that cannot be undone?

Why waste life's precious moments
on things that bruise the heart
when today is ours to fashion
into a work of Art?

Today comes but once, my friend,
it never can return—
so use it wisely while you can,
there's a lesson you may learn.

Let history record the past
and tomorrow come what may.
Be content to do your best
with what you have today!

—Clay Harrison

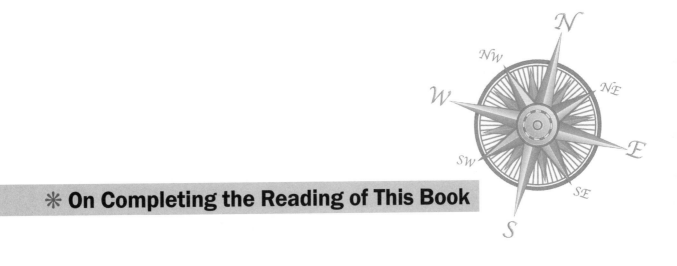

✳ On Completing the Reading of This Book

NOW THAT YOU have finished reading this book, what did you learn about the challenges you will face during your lifetime?

If there are parts of a chapter you didn't understand, reread it or ask someone to explain it.

Keep this book near, so when a question arises anytime in the future, you can quickly refer to the chapter that is germane to the subject.

It is highly recommended that from time to time you reread the chapter on salesmanship. You can never go wrong when you know how to sell.

Wishing you, the reader, all the best in health, wealth, and happiness in the future, I sign off as the author. But I would be amiss if I did not copy this verse from the song "America the Beautiful" by Katharine Lee Bates

O beautiful, for spacious skies,
For amber waves of grain,
For purple mountain majesties,
Above the fruited plain
America, America,
God shed his grace on thee,
And crown thy good, with brotherhood
From sea to shining sea.

If you enjoy reading (and even if you don't), you owe it to yourself to read some or all of the following highly educational books:

- *Shadows of Power* by James Perloff
- *The Creature of Jeykll Island* by G. Edward Griffin
- *Leadership Secrets of Attila the Hun* by Wess Roberts, PhD
- *I'm the Teacher, You're the Student* by Patrick Allit, PhD
- An up-to-date *Webster's Dictionary* for reference: Keep it near you because it is your close and needed friend.

Author's note: I cannot impress upon you, the reader, the importance of increasing your knowledge, as our world shrinks and rivals at home and from abroad will become more competitive in the future.

Only if you can adapt to our changing society and economy will you be able to survive without more knowledge and further education.

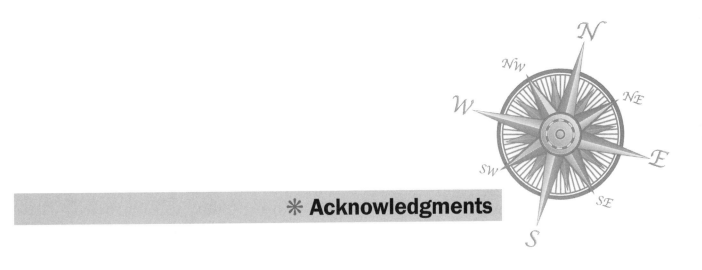

✳ Acknowledgments

I GRATEFULLY ACKNOWLEDGE the following, whose encouraging words helped me in decisions of length and detail of each chapter:

Julie Bakos, grammarian, Naples, Florida

Edwin Blitz, Blitz Financial Services, Northfield, Illinois

James Borden, artist, South Bend, Indiana

Dr. John Brademas, President Emeritus, New York University, New York, New York

Jessica Brazeau, student, Indiana University, South Bend, Indiana

Jacqueline Heinze, editor and proofreader, Portage, Wisconsin

Errett Hicks, assistant, South Bend, Indiana

Gary Houser, artist, Middlebury, Indiana

Dr. John Koumoulides, history professor, Ball State University, Muncie, Indiana

Dr. Thomas Miranda, chemistry professor, Indiana University, South Bend, Indiana

Charles Norton, student, Indiana University, South Bend, Indiana

Richard Reiner, retired banker, South Bend, Indiana

George Roberts, attorney-at-law, South Bend, Indiana

Dr. Herb True, renowned motivational speaker, South Bend, Indiana

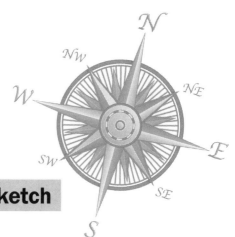

✳ Biographical Sketch

FRANCIS J. BRAZEAU was born August 28, 1921 in the little town of Klondike, Wisconsin, population about twenty-nine or thirty persons, located forty miles north of Green Bay. In April of 1927 my father died, leaving my poor mother with four children and a child born four months after my father died, all younger than I was. My mother sat me down, placed her arm around me, and said, "Francis, you are now the man of the house." I became the babysitter, errand boy, hauler of the coal and kindling wood, plus many other duties. We soon moved to Coleman, Wisconsin, six miles away.

I graduated from high school in 1939, still during the Great Depression, and enrolled in Oshkosh State Teachers College, Oshkosh, Wisconsin, setting pins at the bowling alley to pay my way. My first year in college cost $185 for books, tuition, and room and board.

Suddenly, everything changed on December 7th, 1941. I was in my second year of college, and three or four days later, I was among about twenty-five eager beavers who walked downtown to the recruiting office and signed up. The rest is history. After spending two years in Winfield, Kansas, as a technical sergeant helping to train cadets at Strother Field, I was shipped overseas to get in on the invasion of Normandy, France, on D-Day plus three. After that I joined the 45th Air Depot Group, helping supply our armies with armaments and ammunition, and spent time in France, Belgium, Holland, Germany, England, and Luxembourg. I was in Paris on V-E (Victory-Europe) Day and stood next to General Charles de Gaulle as we celebrated the occasion.

I spent a semester in college in England while in the army of occupation. I had the privilege of being in London on V-J (Victory-Japan) Day. For a young boy from the farm, I can appreciate the WWI song, "How they going to keep them down on the farm after they have seen Paree?"

My service time coming to an end, I boarded an LST (landing ship tank) along with several hundred other GIs, which took us from Le Havre, France, to New York City; then

I took the train home to Coleman. When we landed, all those aboard the ship broke into the song "God Bless America." There wasn't a dry eye to be seen. We were then met by Red Cross ladies, who served us milk and donuts. That was my first drink of fresh milk in almost two years; need I say more?

I drew $5 per month during my time in service, as the Army Air Corps (now the US Air Force) feeds and clothes you. I had saved $5,000, a princely sum of money in those days, and decided to go into business. The die was cast, and I picked the little town of Cambridge to open up a dry cleaning business. Although the town was small, the people were wonderful, and I enjoyed the five years I spent there and was quite successful. Years later I told friends that this experience was the equivalent of a degree at Notre Dame. Wanderlust had caught me, though, so I sold the business and ended up in South Bend, Indiana, where a branch of Indiana University is located.

It was in South Bend at age thirty that I purchased a franchise from the Accounting Corp of America to operate a business service using IBM computer equipment to process work for accounting firms. We were the new kids on the block. Things started to look better all the time, and I joined a group of accountants I was doing business with, and we started a user group. Four years later I became president of this group, and each year we met in different cities, including once in Spain. Life was good, and my wife and I had six daughters. When giving talks at various business groups, I tell them nothing is forever, and I make my point by referring to the fact that at age fifty, after several years of frustration, I left my family, sold the business, and went to work in sales for the Accounting Corp as an independent agent. I took college courses at IU and got real estate, securities, and insurance licenses. This was an interesting sideline, but my love of the computer industry drove me back to become a manager of a service bureau in Detroit; later, I became sales manager for the whole East Coast. In 1986 I retired and moved back to South Bend.

A couple of years later I met the former Eleanor Brademas, who became and still is the love of my life. I have been in forty-nine states and Eleanor in all fifty. We did almost all our travel at home by auto and flew to Europe several times. We live six months in Florida and six in Indiana.

During my business career I was the recipient of several awards: an Honorary Doctor of Letters from the International Free Protestant University, St. Andrews Collegiate Church, London, England; an Honorary Kentucky Colonel from the governor of Kentucky; the Arkansas Traveler award, also from the governor of Kentucky; and many sales awards from the various institutions with which I was affiliated.

I do some public speaking and teach school classes on finances from time to time. I spend as much free time as possible attempting to get drop-out students to return to school and get a diploma.

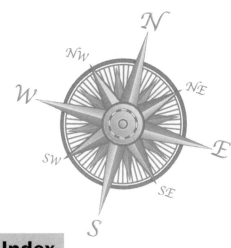

✳ Index

Give the Gift of

The Day after Graduation

What Your Parents and Teachers Did Not Teach You in School
(REVISED EDITION)

to Your Friends and Colleagues

CHECK YOUR LEADING BOOKSTORE OR ORDER HERE

❏ **YES**, I want _____ copies of *The Day after Graduation* at $19.95 each, plus $4.95 shipping per book (Indiana residents please add $1.20 sales tax per book). Canadian orders must be accompanied by a postal money order in U.S. funds. Allow 15 days for delivery.

My check or money order for $_____ is enclosed.

Name _____

Organization _____

Address _____

City/State/Zip _____

Phone_____ Email _____

Card # _____

Exp. Date_____ Signature _____

Please make your check payable and return to:

Circle of Life Books
5223 Monticello Court • South Bend, IN 46614

www.thedayaftergraduation.com

Protecting your students.

Many times you may have students with more enthusiasm than judgement. As they become more knowledgeable, they become more rational and thus more effective. This is the objective of teaching.

When your student tells you what he is doing and is somewhat contrary to what is being taught, take time to correct him after class is over whenever possible or use this data for class discussion.

Attitude towards request for information at your home:

You will have students call you for advice on a number of things. Help them all you can no matter how ambiguous the question (s) may be. If you know the answer can be found in the book, refer them to it in the book. Some students take classes but never do homework, always emphasize the necessity of extra study and you will have less phone calls.

Surveying results

It is a good practice to survey the results of your teaching during the first six or so weeks.

It is suggested you request each student to write his comments or questions on the course thus far. Don't request that they sign them unless they wish. Keep it as objective as possible. This procedure will help you become a better teacher.

Work Sheets and materials:

Go through your chapter and write out questions from the text. Give them to your students after the second week on the first week's chapter. Do this at the beginning of the class. This gives you and your students one week to read and discuss each section.

It also lets the student know that this is a class, not a meeting. You will have knowledgeable enthusiastic students, and upon completion of the semester, a job well done. We highly recommend that the teacher assign 3 students or volunteers to bring other books to class regarding each chapter to get additional thoughts and ideas on each subject.

Affluent students:

Depending on the age of the student, some may have much knowledge on a particular subject. This person may insist on expounding this knowledge unless you keep good control and are ahead of the situation. It may be to your advantage to let the student talk. He can do much good for the class if you interject appropriate comments into his comments.

Often "war stories" can take up valuable time with no contributing element. Control this. You must be prepared to teach. Prepare your presentation each time. Get good at it. Be sure you retain the highest respect for all your students.

Accumulating input:

There will be many suggestions eventually coming from your class. They may be magazine articles or newspaper clippings. Accumulate them and keep the important ones for your class teaching. It is amazing what innovative ideas come from a free mind. The important thing is that you still insist on them learning what is in the book, but not limited to it.

Overcoming fear:

As you have followed your class through a few weeks, you should know which ones are still fearful. Take time to interrogate each one in class in a somewhat subtle fashion. If you do not eliminate fear, it will not make any difference how much you teach. The student will not be able to execute his knowledge. Anyone who is fearful is incapable of clear thought and does not function effectively.

Teaching simplicity:

Never allow your students to assume that what they must learn is complicated. The book is all about life and all of us are about life and how we will handle it after we graduate. Take one example: INSURANCE. Once they understand it and put into practice, they will save thousands of dollars over a lifetime.

Conclusion:

Establish the objective of this class. Be sure you sum up the intent of the chapter, so that each student walks out knowing much more about the subject matter and its applicability. It is sometimes wise to write the goal on the blackboard that you wish to reach, so that all students will have it in mind. This also keeps the teacher and the student from straying off the subject.

Chapter 1 – Learning – Page 15

Teacher should read pages 16 - 19

Students take the self analysis questions and discuss with the teacher. Keeping your test scores for a repeat test a few months later, can help you improve your weak points.

Teacher: Discuss the 1895 exam. Don't expect any of them to pass, but it should be an eye opener for all. Pages 26, 27 and 28.

Class reading and discussion pages 31 through 38.

Teacher: In talking to businessmen I was told the two biggest problems they found when interviewing potential employees was Attitude and Dress. What should be a home run on an interview in the majority of time turns out to be a disaster. Applicants poorly dressed , men wearing earrings, baseball cap with brim in back does not make a good impression. Women applying for an office position with typing speed under fifty words per minute, and poor manners constitute a negative impression. This could and should entail at least one full class period.

Chapter 2 – Selling – Page 40

Student: Pages 40 through 47. Study this chapter as if your life depended on it, it probably does. Whether you are 16 or 60, join Toastmasters and/or Dale Carnegie. or any other sales organization. You will learn so much from your instructor and your peers, and a plus will be in making new and in many cases lasting friends.

Chapter 2 – Page 48 – Sales Demonstrations

Hours of planning, hours, maybe weeks of testing, hours of rehearsing will be lost if your timing is off, so allow yourself and assistants plenty of time to make certain everything runs smoothly.

After you have made your sales pitch and do not make a sale, review all the things you did (or didn't do), to attempt to find out why your prospect didn't buy.

A quick example, (my own experience): I was selling life insurance to a veteran of World War II, and he politely listened to my demonstration. He didn't buy. My

analysis later showed me, "he didn't need it." He had a pension for life and had inherited a sizeable estate. Answer: I didn't do my homework to find this out in advance, rather than later.

Chapter 3 – Personal Financial Planning -- Pages 55 thru 66

Teacher: In speaking to individuals and groups, I am finding in many cases complete ignorance regarding the business world. We have college students who have never written a check and thus never balanced a checking account. They have no idea what insurance is all about, have never saved one nickel, and yet feel they are old enough to get married and start a family. I recommend that after your students have finished all nine chapters, you do a review of all the chapters, but especially chapters 2 & 3. This is a lifetime educational gift that will never go out of style.

Teacher: Page 55 – Quote Benjamin Franklin
Thousands of people who didn't or couldn't save would not be on welfare today if they read this one sentence and followed his advice.

In life you must have a goal (s). Saving money is an absolute must if you are to have things you want. Forget the lottery as very few ever win and those that do spend it like there is no tomorrow.
Page 58 – Give each student a copy of this sample cash flow chart or the equivalent thereof. Question: how will they know where their money went if they do not keep track?

Teacher: Plastic money -- Page 60
For the most part, credit cards are bad, but the interest these banditos are allowed to charge is a disgrace. Probably more bankruptcies are the result of these little pieces of plastic than any other reason.
Teacher: No Free Lunch – Page 61
Author comments: "My two favorite expressions are {attitude and no free lunch}"
There are very few winners that have a poor attitude and there isn't any free lunch, period.

Teacher: Page 62 – Starting a savings plan and learning about compounding interest

        Study the chart on page 63

Teacher: Depending on whether you are teaching an individual, a high school or college student, pages 65 and 66 give you a quick peek at what is ahead for most students, maybe not today but soon.

Chapter 4 – Investing For Your Future

Teacher: This chapter brings insurance, investing and saving although they also have individual chapters. The financial business place has several homes. Pages 67-76

Once your students learn the Rule of 72, page 72, they should remember it for life and start saving ASOP, no ifs ands or buts. The American Dream on page 74 tells all.

Chapter 5 – Insurance – Page 77

Teacher: This chapter is probably the most difficult to understand. So read, and reread it, and ask someone with more knowledge on this subject. Insurance agents don't always agree on the subject matter, but I have spent many hours on this and feel you will enjoy what you learned about it. Keep in mind, all insurance is term or term plus. Study the three legged stool because if you follow it, you should end up financially O.K.

Chapter 6 – Health Page 87

Teacher: Everything in Moderation (EIM) – Page 88

Here is that three legged stool again, Dress-Attitude-Communication. If these three are in sync, all should be well. Ask the question, "why?" – Page 89

Chapter 7 – Decisions, Decisions – Page 91

Teacher: suggest you have each student read this chapter and then write a short paragraph on the toughest decision they have ever had to make and was it successful or unsuccessful?

Have them participate in a problem that requires deep thought. An example might be: What you have to do with your pet when you go to school, or your pet needs to be put to sleep or given away. For some the decision is easy, for an animal lover, it becomes a heart-wrenching time in your life. Now each student should make their own tough decision.

Chapter 8 – Wills and Living Trusts -- Page 95

Will your will be done? This is a rather humorous example of what may happen to someone's wishes after they pass on.

Teacher : The fact that we are all going to meet our maker sooner or later, begs each of you to look down the road of life. More than half the people die without making their final arrangements. Will any of you sitting here be one of them?

A true story: It was Christmas time in Oklahoma City. OK some years ago. Christmas parties were taking place everywhere. A senator from Oklahoma came back from Washington, D.C. to help celebrate the occasion and while there talked to his long time friend and attorney. The senator mentioned to the attorney his need for making a last will and testament. The attorney nodded in agreement and said. "Stop by my office the first of the year and we will do just that." Case closed. Not yet! You see the senator pasted on over the weekend with the resulting problems facing the heirs. With no will, the heirs shares had to be divided with the state of Oklahoma and attorney fees and thus

lost millions of what would have been theirs instead. Reread this chapter again and then do something or do nothing.

- Chapter 9 : The Good Life – page 103

We all want it but about 95% of our population never seems to get it.

Teacher: This chapter, a potpourri of expressions, sayings, quotations and miscellaneous subjects guided me throughout my life, and I wish to share them with all my readers. There are many lessons in life so I picked both funny and serious ones. Read, enjoy and quote from them. The older you get, the more you should enjoy them.

My favorite is on pages 125, 126, 127 and 128.

Teacher: friends and other readers tell me, that you must read this book two or more times to really appreciate all these lessons in life.

The mediocre teacher tells, the good teacher explains, the superior teacher demonstrates, the great teacher inspires. by William Arthur Ward

A good teacher, like a good entertainer first must hold his audience's attention. Then he can . teach his lesson. by John Hendrik Clarke

Teach your student to have an up-to-date dictionary near him every time he picks up a book.

It is hard to convince a high school student that he will encounter a lot of problems more difficult than those of algebra and geometry. by Edward. W. Howe

We expect teachers to handle teen age pregnancy, substance abuse, and family failings. Then we expect them to educate our children. by John Sculley

Try to start your class with an expression, a poem, an interesting story or news event, discuss it as your opening thoughts and get the class thinking. Fjb

Finale thought....keep things rolling. Fjb

12-01/09